## ABOUT THE AUTHOR

On a lonely, rainswept battlefield in the South Pacific during World War II, Harry Douglas Smith witnessed a miracle of healing that changed his life forever. In that thrilling hour, he had a vision of the Infinite Power that pervades the Universe—and, in the years that followed, one Great Truth after another was revealed to him, convincing him beyond the shadow of a doubt of the enormous power and universal range of this mighty Force for good.

From that day on, he dedicated his life to helping men and women in all walks of life make personal contact with that great Power. He founded, and became Director and Minister of the Church of Life in Hollywood, California where, every Sunday morning, his audience would exceed a thousand people. His regular radio broadcasts were closely followed by hundreds of thousands of listeners.

Since then, he witnessed hundreds of miraculous healings—healings which, in many cases, science simply *could not explain*—healings achieved under his personal direction and through the use of the principles explained in this book.

4

0-13-797936-3

# the
# SECRET
## of
# INSTANTANEOUS
# HEALING

*Every man who knows how to read has it in his power to magnify himself, to multiply the ways in which he exists, to make his life full, significant and interesting.*

—ALDOUS HUXLEY

# the
# SECRET
# of
# INSTANTANEOUS
# HEALING

## Harry Douglas Smith

West Nyack
New York

PARKER
PUBLISHING
COMPANY, Inc.

PRINTED IN THE UNITED STATES OF AMERICA
79795—B&P

# What You Can Attain
# if You Use This Book Properly

In the quietness of your own home, in the silence of your own thoughts you will find an instantaneous Healing Power. In this book you will find the secrets of using that power.

Have you ever complained about your circumstances, the conditions that surround you, the things you lack in life, the dreams that never were fulfilled, the recurrent illnesses and troubles that plague you? Perhaps so. The world is full of complaints. But your days or years of complaints can be over. This book gives you the secrets of freeing yourself from unwanted circumstances and conditions, from the troubles and illnesses that have battered and beaten your body, your mind, and your affairs. Moreover, it tells you—in that quietness and silence, in the privacy of your own consciousness—how *to make these secrets work for YOU.*

When you finish this book, no longer will you be among those men and women in this world who have lost faith in themselves, who have no confidence in their own power, and little hope for healing.

### Just One Thought Away

There are those whose dreams are always frustrated, whose great ambitions are always crushed, and whose happiness and health, at best, are never more than second-rate. Why? Because they underestimate the power of their own minds. Twenty, thirty, forty, fifty, sixty, seventy years go by, while the power that is only *one thought away* is never quite called into action.

In this book you will find some suggestions that may be found in other places. Here, however, they have been assembled and organized to make your search for health *successful*. Here you also will find suggestions that will be completely new to you, that you will *not* find elsewhere, and that will add a tremendous new dimension to *your* life. Throughout this book there will be one important ingredient that so often is lacking in all the other approaches to illness and its healing. Here you will find spiritual overtones and undertones. This means that the value of this book for you will be multiplied many times if, whatever your personal religious convictions may or may not be, you are led to conclude:

1. that there *is* an Infinite Creative Intelligence,
2. that you are a part of that Intelligence, and
3. that you never can be separated from it.

God and your experiences are indivisible, whether you know it, want it, or wish to believe it.

Here, then, you will find the means of making yourself receptive to the action of God in you, the Creative, Healing Power that already is a part of you. Once you have followed the suggestions and directions given here, you are subject to the INSTANTANEOUS HEALING of *any* illness or disease.

### If You Are Searching for Healing, Your Search Begins and Ends Here

This book is for those who sincerely are searching for healing. It is for those who are ready to recognize that they are channels for an Infinite Healing Power, even though they are not the exclusive possessors of that power.

For such men and women, and I assume *you* are one of them, this book will divulge the secrets that can lead to INSTANTANE-OUS HEALING and to a way of life in which *health is the natural, normal, lifetime condition it was meant to be.*

### How to Use This Book

This is more than just another inspirational book. It is a source book on the major principles of healing and health. Read it as quickly or as slowly as you wish, but do not hurry it. There are a certain number of ideas for you to understand, some suggestions for you to follow, and truths to accept. Your speed of reading is entirely your own concern. It depends only upon how well you follow the directions for each day (and each chapter) as you read. Do not let your *reading* get beyond your *doing.*

For the *Evening* of the first day after you have finished the first chapter you will be given some ideas for your subconscious mind to dwell upon during the night while you are asleep. This is an easy practice, for you will need only think of those ideas and let them be, as nearly as you can, the last ideas you think of before you go to sleep.

To match these *Evening* ideas or thoughts, you will be given some *Morning* thoughts. These will be for two purposes:

1. to correct any errors or negative patterns of your past subconscious night, and
2. to set the tone for your life for the remainder of that day by giving you fresh, healing ideas soon after you awaken.

These two groups of thoughts end your first day and begin the next.

You will be given a third group of thoughts for the *Day* itself.

These three simple groups will carry you through your entire day from the moment of waking to the moment of sleeping. They also will protect you from any possible conflicts and difficulties on the subconscious level of life while your conscious mind is asleep.

You are not to "work" at these thoughts. Make your contemplation of them as effortless as possible. They are *healing* thoughts, not those to give you any sense of study or hardship. They have only one purpose: *to make you well, and to keep you well.*

### Your Healing Idea Cards—
### What They Are and How to Use Them

You will need a total of 48 3 x 5 white cards, or something similar, on which to write the various statements or thoughts given at the end of each chapter throughout this book. They are your means of putting a secret of healing into action.

Use one card for the *Morning* thoughts, one card for the *Day* thoughts, and one card for the *Evening* thoughts. This means that you will have only three cards for each full day. Turn the cards over and write on the back if you need more room.

If it is more convenient, and you can carry the book with you, you need only mark the pages of the Ideas with slips of paper for quick and easy reference.

### What to Do With the Cards

EVENING: When you have written (or marked in the book) the ideas for the evening, read them quietly and carefully as the last thing you do before going to sleep. If you lie in bed with the lights off, and find you are not going to sleep immediately, keep thinking quietly and easily of the ideas you have read. Repeat them to yourself. Put them into your own words. You do not need to memorize them. In this way you will be giving your subconscious mind these creative, healing thoughts to work with during the night, instead of the usual worried, fearful, confused ones. Do not use the moments or hours before sleep to review all your problems, troubles, and illnesses. Think only of the ideas on your cards.

MORNING: Place these cards near your bed so that you may read them and think about them when you first wake up. If you prefer, put them around your shaving or makeup mirror where you can see and read them while you are getting ready for the day. Or you may take them to breakfast with you and read them there. If you are married, it would be best to read the cards earlier, unless you share them with your husband or your wife at breakfast. Whatever time or place you choose, make it so that you can read without interruption from someone else or a feeling that you should be doing something else. But whatever you do, fill your mind with the messages of the card before your day really begins.

DAY: When you have made the Idea Cards for this period, put them in the pocket of your dress or suit, or in the handbag or briefcase you will be carrying that day. Do not simply put them there and forget them. During the day take whatever opportunities present themselves to glance at the cards and to read all or part of their messages. Make them a part of your conscious thoughts for that day, and, above all, *try to make your day fit the thoughts!* If any other thoughts or circumstances come to you that seem in conflict with the card thoughts for that day, reject them as having no authority, meaning, influence, or reality for you. For instance, you may say about something that is contrary to what you are reading on your card:

*This is not true for me. I reject it. It does not belong to me. I refuse to believe or to accept anything which is opposed to the ideas of health and wholeness, happiness and peace I am now reading and choosing for myself.*

During the day be alert to everything that will *confirm* the ideas expressed on your card or cards. Look for *them*, not for those ideas, circumstances, or experiences that may be in conflict with them. Do not allow your thoughts or conversations at any time during the day to dwell on anything that is not in agreement with the creative, positive principles stated on your cards.

In other words, you are beginning to *live* the thoughts you are reading.

As you progress through the days, the number of your cards will increase. Keep all the Morning cards together, all the Day cards together, and all the Evening cards together. For the best use of this book, read one chapter a day.

Always concentrate most on the last day's cards you have written, but at the same time re-read all the previous ones at the appropriate times (morning, day, evening) when it can be done without any sense of it being "too much."

By the time you finish this book you will have 16 sets of 3 cards each, or a total of 48 cards (or corresponding marked places in the book).

*Live* with these ideas. Make them part of you. Use the cards until you are familiar with all the healing ideas they contain, and until you are applying them to every activity of your life.

*Then*—compare the life you are *enjoying* with the one you
may only have been *suffering!*

# Contents

14

*Contents*

# 1

# How Instantaneous Healing
# Can Restore, Protect, and
# Preserve Your Health

Fifty million buffalo, in four great herds, once roamed the American West. Surviving every threat, they remained the strongest single animal group on the North American continent until man, through carelessness, thoughtlessness, and wanton destruction, brought them to the point of extinction. Only then, realizing the possibility that the buffalo might be lost forever, did man take steps to preserve the less than 250 that remained. The preservation of the buffalo had suddenly become important.

In 35 B.C., a seedling redwood began life in the coastal ranges of California. It was a member of the world's oldest and largest family of living organisms. For two thousand years it overcame fire, flood, fungus, insects, and storm. But a man walked up to it one day, and cut it down. The same thoughtlessness, carelessness, and wanton destruction that threatened the buffalo, was now turned against the redwoods. Once again, only when man began to see that he alone was bringing the giant groves toward extinction, did he realize how important they were, and only then did he take steps to preserve them.

17

The agriculturally rich states of Kansas, Oklahoma, and Texas became one huge "dust bowl" in the 1930's because man, wanting to use the land for all it was worth, did not think to safeguard that land with soil conservation, cover crops, erosion protection, and contour plowing. Thoughtlessness, carelessness, and ignorance laid waste vast areas of America's grazing and farm lands. The health of the land disappeared. Only then did methods to preserve and restore the land seem important.

The life of the giant redwoods, the strength and numbers of the buffalo, the health of the land were dangerously threatened, almost destroyed by the thoughtlessness of man. Only when he was about to lose them did he remember their importance. How often our great natural resources, seemingly unending and inexhaustible, are suddenly depleted, and come close to being lost forever! Because of their strength, their health, and their numbers, we have taken them for granted. We have become the wastrels, prodigal of our blessings, until, alarmed, we take measures to correct our thoughtlessness and destruction.

### Don't Treat Your Health the Same Way

Just as we did with the buffalo, the redwoods, and the land, so do we often treat *another great natural resource—our own health.*

How often it, too, so abundant at one time, has been squandered, neglected, unprotected, limited, forgotten. How often so ruthlessly spent in our hurry to get things, when suddenly we realize it is going, or gone. And then, in panic, we search for restoration and conservation methods we once thought so unimportant.

So many of us take our health for granted while it is here, then desperately try to recall it once it is gone. Like the white men who came out of the East, our emotions pour out from the beginnings of our desires, armed with all the latest gadgets to speed us on our way toward ever greater pressure, tension, deadlines. Like those who slaughtered the buffalo and ravished the forest, we level against the natural resource of our health all the weapons of destructive attitudes we can muster.

Are we, in truth, individually wasting this greatest of our natural resources—our health? Has it been useful, but otherwise so unimportant to us that we can be as careless of it as we were with the buffalo, the redwoods, and the land?

### Recognize the Enemies of Your Health

There is nothing dramatic in ruining our health by destructive emotions and beliefs. The battles, while deadly, usually are hidden. Often we try to dramatize our illnesses, however, by attributing them to many false things.

We fail to realize that the *spirit* of hundreds of thousands of men and women is being felled with the axe of fear, hatred, irritation, overload, burden, and worry.

We do not see that the strength of millions is being sapped by anger, jealousy, bitterness, impatience, futility; that the resilience, the snap, the quick reflexes are becoming slow and flabby under the constant attrition of guilt, inadequacy, indecision, and procrastination.

We refuse to recognize or acknowledge that the vast potentials and power we once had have become decimated by the carelessness of our own thoughts.

We forget that the protective covering of faith has been blown away by the winds of spiritual ignorance rising within our own consciousness.

We buy insurance; we get accident, sickness, and disability coverage; we join the "crisis clubs," and subscribe to hospital plans. Then we sit back and nonchalantly say, "Well, if I get sick, I'm taken care of."

But what do we do to protect, to preserve, to conserve the health we have? Is it no more important than an insurance premium, a pass into a clinic, a room at the hospital? Is it no more important than a guarantee that if we get sick we'll "be taken care of"?

If we are wiser than those who waited to get concerned until the buffalo, the trees, and the top-soil became almost extinct, we shall—well or ill—recognize the importance of our health *now,* and do something *now* to preserve or to reclaim it.

First, it is a matter of decision. Just as we must make some decision regarding the car we buy, the television programs we watch, the clothes we wear, the houses we live in, we must make some decisions about our health. For the sake of the INSTANTANEOUS HEALING we may so desire, what shall we keep, and what discard in our own consciousness, our own thinking? For our health's sake, what shall we do, how shall we think, by what means shall we eliminate the sickening influences in our lives? This book gives the answers.

Some persons go through life attracting illness, physical imbalance, weakness, and fatigue without knowing it. They think the risk of such things is to be expected if one is to live this life at all. They are the spendthrifts, the squanderers of their own God-given natural resource.

Nevertheless,

> If our health is gone, it can be *restored.*
> If our health is threatened, it can be *protected.*
> If it is perfectly good, it can be *preserved.*

A simple method, outlined in the next few chapters, makes restoration, protection, and preservation possible for everyone.

It means, however, giving up some things and acquiring others. It demands consistency of purpose and action, and finally, dedication of both time and thought. If you are willing to do and give these things, INSTANTANEOUS HEALING can be yours.

### Don't Wait Until You Are Desperate

Don't make the mistake of supposing that the steps and principles given in this book are written only for you to refer to when you are desperate, and that they are rather useless when your health is good. This was the attitude of those men who forgot conservation methods until a crisis occurred, but who now recognize and practice such methods so that no further crisis will appear.

Once again,

constantly to remind us of this

both human and spiritual conservation method,

to help us regain our health,

to save it when it is threatened, and

to protect it while it is here,

these are among the major purposes of this book.

Already you have made some progress. The next chapter will help you overcome some old ideas that have made the restoration, the protection, and the preservation of health seem more difficult than they really are.

### Make Your Cards, or Mark This Place

Here is the first set of your *Healing Ideas*. You will note that the cards you will make for each chapter begin with the ones for *Evening*, follow with the ones for *Morning*, and continue with others for the *Day*.

A new chapter (with a new set of ideas) begins after you have finished another chapter or chapters. You may work with one chapter at a time, or with several at once, depending upon the speed of your reading and comprehension.

Now—get three cards.

Label one *Evening*,

one *Morning*,

and one *Day*.

Write, type, or print on them the ideas below, and use them

as you were instructed in "What You Can Attain if You Use This Book Properly," or mark this place in the book for easy reference.

•-•-•-•-•-•-•-•-•-•-•-•-•-•-•-•-•-•-•-•-•-•-•-•-•-•-•-•-•-•-•-•

### EVENING

*I give thanks for that part of health I have expressed today.*
*I know that, in ways I cannot even see, it is increasing.*
*Tonight, as I sleep, my subconscious mind will work on this idea:*
> *I am whole, healthy, perfect.*
> *Every negative, fearful, destructive idea has been thrown out of my mind and life.*

•-•-•-•-•-•-•-•-•-•-•-•-•-•-•-•-•-•-•-•-•-•-•-•-•-•-•-•-•-•-•-•

### MORNING

*I give thanks for a night in which my body received some unknown healing power while I was asleep.*
*I look forward to this new day in which I shall find new evidence of my returning health.*
*Today I keep my thoughts clear and free of all negative, destructive ideas.*
*My whole being is open and receptive to happiness, strength, and peace.*

•-•-•-•-•-•-•-•-•-•-•-•-•-•-•-•-•-•-•-•-•-•-•-•-•-•-•-•-•-•-•-•

### DAY

*I will not dramatize or repeat any stories of my illness today.*
*I will not cut down my own body by careless thinking.*
*I will neither listen to nor join in destructive conversations.*
*My health is important to me NOW.*
> *Therefore I respect and protect it NOW.*
*By my careful, creative thinking today I am*
> *restoring,*
> *protecting, and*
> *preserving my HEALTH.*

•-•-•-•-•-•-•-•-•-•-•-•-•-•-•-•-•-•-•-•-•-•-•-•-•-•-•-•-•-•-•-•

# 2

## Why You're Wrong
## When You Think You
## Can't Be Helped

The next few paragraphs will explain one of the most basic truths you will find in this book. Read them carefully. What you read may propose ideas entirely new to you. They may seem incredible, even fantastic. But they will be the means—not only of your understanding and acceptance of the principles of this book—but of leading you easily and effortlessly to the application of those principles which will make your INSTANTANEOUS HEALING possible.

There are many men and women who would deny that they ever resort to prayer. But whether they know it or not, they never stop praying.

*Every thought is a prayer. Every thought infused with belief is an answered prayer.*

Why? Because every thought is somehow a communication between the mind of man and the mind of God. It is impossible to have a thought without that thought having its "Listener" on the Infinite level. We have been told that we are all made in the image and likeness of God. Our minds are only extensions

23

of the one Infinite Mind. We think, we create, we experience by using that mind in us on the human level, by transmuting the *Infinite* experience into our own *individual* experience.

When we think, we pray. A prayer does not have to be a *conscious* prayer. Prayers can be negative or positive, creative or destructive, just as the thoughts which engender them. It is important to know this, because when we infuse these thoughts with our *belief*, they become *answered* prayer.

*Fear* is one of our strongest beliefs. A thought infused with fear begins to be answered on the fear level. Job recognized this ancient truth when he said, "That which I feared has come upon me." (Job 3:25.) However, it is not the specific thing feared which must always be manifested. We experience something which corresponds to the intensity or quality of our fear, whether or not that experience is exactly the thing or experience we feared.

Once you accept the idea that when you think, you really are praying, you will be like the woman who said, when she discovered this, that thereafter she was going to "think twice before thinking once." At any rate, remember this sentence: *Think as if your life depends upon it, because it does!*

### You Can Avoid Unwanted Experiences

We constantly are praying our way into happiness or sorrow, health or illness. This is because we think, because we are creatures of emotions and beliefs. Our bodies and our affairs are simply *reflections* of our thoughts, emotions and beliefs. This will be explained and illustrated in later chapters. It is asked that for the moment, at least, you accept it.

It must follow, then, that if we can pray our way *into* these conditions, we can also pray our way *out* of them. The progress or the deterioration of our bodies and affairs need not follow a one-way street. All we need to know is how to think *creatively*— in other words, how to *pray* creatively. Every chapter is designed to make it easier and more natural for you to do just this.

Forget the old concept of prayer as an act of pleading with God, or a conscious turning to the Supreme Power in fear and supplication. These are only limitations on the word "prayer." We *do* pray when we plead with God, but the very fact that we are pleading infuses the prayer with the belief that denial is possible. We *do* pray when we turn to God in fear or supplication, but these again become the prayers of doubt, and the presence of doubt demonstrates that what we *think* has greater power than what we *want*.

You cannot imagine *any* thoughts which are not prayers in the true sense of the word. Therefore, it becomes increasingly urgent for you to correct and improve your thinking so that you are not—through your fears, doubts, and negative beliefs—attracting the *unwanted answers*, and the *unwanted experiences*.

### How to Use the Word "Treatment"

In order to free ourselves from the old connotations which cling to the word *prayer,* we shall occasionally use a different word. That word is treatment. It is intended that this word suggest to us a conscious realization that whenever we *think*, we are *praying;* therefore our thoughts should always be on the highest level possible so that *through* those prayers (through our thoughts), we are giving ourselves what may be called a *creative treatment* rather than a haphazard, hit-or-miss, indecisive, and destructive one.

Furthermore, because I can think of you, I can "treat" for you, just as you may "treat" for me. There is no limitation in time or space to a thought. The communication system for my thought is the same as that for yours. We are all part of the one system. My healing treatment for you (my healing or creative thoughts about you) is directed in and through that one Infinite Power of which each of us is a part. And because you, too, are a part of it, it reaches you and has a healing effect on you, whether you are consciously aware of it or not.

I explain all this in order to make it clear that when someone across the desk, in a letter, or on the other end of a telephone line asks me to treat for him or for her, or to treat for a loved one a thousand or ten thousand miles away, I do so through my knowledge of these truths. I do so successfully *only* in the awareness of the truths which are revealed in this book. This makes it possible for me to treat without doubt, with complete faith, and with instant effectiveness.

To some persons life is a chase. They are chasing happiness, while trouble is chasing them. Too often trouble wins. They feel trapped, pinned to the wall, cornered in some tragic cul-de-sac. They break down, give up, resign themselves. Pleasure loses its punch. Life loses its zest. Happiness becomes only heartbreak and disillusion. Such men and women tell themselves that they can't be helped, that they are "beyond hope."

The most effective block to any kind of healing is the belief that one cannot be helped. Even the suspicion of hopelessness is dangerous. Anyone who allows himself to slip into this frame of mind is, in truth, asking for what he fears, and preparing to accept what he doesn't want.

To claim that our situation is hopeless, to affirm that there is no place to turn, to believe in our ultimate defeat, to give power to some negative idea or destructive force, is to deny the existence of an ever-present help that men of insight and wisdom have known and used for centuries.

### Healing Is Everywhere

True healing, while not necessarily a common occurrence, nevertheless is a world-wide experience. Every culture, society, and religion can point to so-called miraculous healings. There always have been instances in which some fortuitous combination of circumstance and state of mind has resulted in someone's healing. No one possesses an exclusive healing power. There are no cultural, geographic, time, business, religious, or ethnic limitations to possible healing.

However, by the very fact that healings are not common, that millions of men and women fail every year to achieve victory over their illnesses and diseases, we are reminded that healing does not come simply because we want it to come. To be healed of an illness is one of the most desperately sought-after experiences in the whole history of man, yet one of the most elusive. Obviously, then, there is some secret, some uncommon knowledge that this book reveals. Each paragraph, each line you have been reading has been opening just a little more of this secret to you.

The word *secret* is not used in the sense that it is some closely guarded, esoteric, exclusive information, but only to point out that the vast majority of the world's men and women have failed to learn what has always been theirs to learn. This book is written to dispel some of the mystery that has surrounded healing, and to make the experience elusive no longer.

### How You Heal Yourself

The secret is revealed a bit more when we come to accept the truth that we do not heal the cause of our illnesses merely by dosing or cutting out the effects. The causes of every effect begin in the mind. *It is to avoid this realization* that so many never get beyond the first part of the secret. They cannot bring themselves to believe or to admit that the cause of their illness does not lie "out there" somewhere, but within themselves.

It is true, of course, that many healings have been achieved by those who have never even suspected this truth. For a healing to be permanent, however, this truth must be known, understood, and acted upon. The mind must be cleared of its negative and destructive attitudes, beliefs, and emotions, or illness again will break through into life.

## The Atmosphere in Which Healing and Health Are Yours

The truly healthy mind, reflected in the truly healthy body, is the mind centered on God-like principles, the mind which does not drop or drift to the levels of thinking that are, in themselves, sick. The spiritually-oriented mind, the God-conscious mind, remains above the sick levels of thinking, and thus above the manifestations of such sickness in the body. There is no illness in God. The Infinite is not headachy, sniffly, arthritic, rheumatic, or pain-wracked. Therefore, health is maintained by maintaining the mind, and hence the body, in a God-like atmosphere, and healing is achieved by bringing that mind, and hence the body, up *to* that God-like atmosphere. This does not mean simply being "good," avoiding "sin," or burying oneself in a cloister away from temptation. Rather, it means living a constructive, active life according to the strong, creative, positive principles outlined in this book.

Therefore, whatever you read here, whatever suggestions you find here, whatever secrets are revealed here, you will be aware of spiritual over-tones and under-tones, for these things are done in the knowledge that whatever else may be in doubt, there is no question but that "In God we live, and move, and have our being." (Romans 8:31.)

## The Art of Healing Is Yours to Learn

Because he thinks, man so often gets himself into a predicament from which he must be rescued. Because of its ignorance, or fear, his own mind leads him into error. Catastrophe threatens. Retreat is cut off. The past is irretrievable. Escape is blocked. The future holds only terror, suffering, emptiness, and loneliness. He searches desperately for something to save him, something in which he does not even believe, something he doubts, mistrusts, and is sure will be unable to help him. All his faith deserts him. Sickness overcomes his courage. Resignation envelopes his hope. Although he may get others to cry with him, to cower with him into some spiritless corner of life—although he may surround himself with sympathy, attracting looks of pity and words of compassion—he will find that these are only companions of his misery, rather than agents of his salvation. He may sing his songs of thanksgiving. He may pray his prayers of hope. He may tell himself that faith is a wonderful thing, and that he is glad he has plenty of it. But when a real challenge comes, how often the prayer seems hollow, the music a mockery. It is then that he is in danger of deserting the very thing which stands ready to save him.

How much like such a man many of us are! Despite our words, our songs, and our protestations, some of us really believe that trouble is right on our heels, that the chase is on, and that we dare not stumble, we dare not take the wrong turn, because if we do, we'll have to surrender, or turn and fight alone.

The difficulty in these instances is that when we feel weak, we judge the healing power of the Infinite by that weakness. When are we going to realize that the power to heal everything is not a personal talent that we develop as we would the talent to paint? The power to heal everything is a universal, infinite, unlimited, unbounded power. We may learn the art of using it, as we shall in this book, but we cannot weaken it simply because we do *not* use it.

The would-be suicide who stares at a bottle of sleeping-pills—
The discouraged businessman who faces bankruptcy—
The frightened woman who has just had a threatening diagnosis from her doctor—
The person whose spirit is shredded from the stabs of loneliness—
The woman whose loss of a loved one has undermined her whole world—

The young man who feels rejected, useless, unwanted—
The young woman who wasn't prepared for the demands of
  life—
The old man who looks back with bitterness and regret—
Those who fear the unnamed, unknown, faceless, formless
  terrors of tomorrow—

all these, and any more you can think of, need never believe that they can't be helped. They are wrong when they think they are beyond hope, past saving, too late for salvation. They are underestimating the Infinite, discrediting God, disputing the Creator by thinking that although the miraculous has touched and healed the lives of others, *they* are unique; *they* are different, and untouchable; *they* have been forgotten, and stand facing the "enemy" naked and alone. They are wrong!

### It Worked for Them—It Will Work for You

I have never seen and never expect to see anyone, no matter how serious his situation or condition may be, who could not be helped.

"There was no way out," said a letter I received from a man in San Francisco, "but I found it just the same. Two months ago I didn't see how I could live. I didn't even want to live. But I found my reason for living and my power to live through you. It isn't the same world any more."

Let it be clear right now that the healing relationship between the one who is ill or is in trouble, and the one who helps him become well or to rise above his trouble, is the same as the relationship between you who are reading this book, and the book itself. Whenever I have been called upon to work with or for anyone, I have applied the same principles of healing that you are learning in this book. In your case, *because you have this book,* there will be no need for the "middle man" in achieving your healing.

A father and mother see their little boy on the verge of death. The doctors offer no hope. All the signs indicate the end. The parents give up. Nothing can help them now. But the grandmother refuses to accept the human verdict. She has made friends with the silent Source of all our help. She asks for that help. Here, a few days later, is what she writes.

> I am so happy to say that on Wednesday everything changed for the better. Here it is only Friday, and we can scarcely keep him down. He is so full of energy, and is our smiling, happy boy again. I feel certain that if we hadn't had God's help, our little boy would not be with us today. The doctors couldn't get over the resistance he had. I only wish I could have been there to tell them it was God's help.

Through her treatment and ours we claimed for this boy all the things and conditions this book will teach you to claim for yourself.

Another woman who had faced a crisis wrote this:

> At 4:00 P.M. today, the problem we were working on looked hopeless. At 4:30 P.M. it was answered in a most unexpected way.

In half-an-hour the answer came. Only one thought away, in the consciousness of each one of us, is the healing answer for all our ills.

> When you had compassion deep enough to perform miracles, it gave me another reason to thank this scientific philosophy you teach and believe, and which I am trying to know, for uprooting life-long convictions, and to induce me to consider the promise, "There is no death." I called you at 9:30 this morning, very ill, aching unbearably, and with a mind too heavy to think except to fear that this was it. I slept until 10:30. When I awoke I was free, entirely at ease, my mind clear. It was the most

peculiar and unbelievable experience I've had in my whole life.

My part in her miracle? Accepting for her the condition of health that she was too weak, too worried, and too sick to claim and accept for herself. When she allowed me to take over for her, I impressed upon her subconscious the direct and instant power of thought flowing from my mind to hers. I claimed the eight steps to healing as already completed for her, and it was done. This method of healing—using the conviction, knowledge and faith in one mind to heal the fears and errors in another—has been called Spiritual Treatment, as discussed earlier, but these words are used only to denote the more scientific approach to the ancient practice of prayer.

A man called me by telephone from Chicago. He was desperate. A friend of his had told him of our work. He couldn't believe that anything we could say or do would help him. Nevertheless, he called. He was afraid our "religion" (the quotes were his, obvious even in conversation) wouldn't work. He was afraid *his* religion wouldn't approve. What difference, I asked him, so long as we know the source of our power, does our "religion" make to God? There are no denominational fences circling the provinces of the Infinite. Such fences are only the limitations which humanity places on its own consciousness.

I asked him what he wanted. He explained his condition. "But I don't think anybody can help me," he said.

"You are not going to be helped by anyone," I told him. "But you are going to be helped through someone, and that someone may as well be me."

I explained that he must not turn to me as an "intercessor" between him and God, but as one who, having dedicated himself to understanding and applying the healing laws of God, could cooperate with him in getting him back into harmony with those laws. He had begged in his own prayers, but begging demonstrates a poverty of faith. He had pleaded with God, but pleading demonstrates a suspicion of refusal. We changed that. He united his consciousness with mine by agreeing to work in this way with me, and to be receptive to all help that would come to him. I united *our* consciousness with the unfailing Source of every answer. The healing power was now at work. He accepted the idea that he could be, and would be, well. The help that *men* could not give was given.

Subsequently, he has called me to confer on minor problems several times over the past two years. But now it is not in desperation; it is with the knowledge that help is available. He has studied and applied what you are studying and will apply. His doubt has changed to confidence. His faith has been renewed. His methods have been corrected and redirected. It is no longer with a sense of guilt, with a feeling of having cheated on his own religion, that he seeks this means of help. He knows now that terms do not frighten God, that man is not sanctified by organizations, and that help is not held in trust, nor doled out by a cartel for a selected few.

Hereafter, when *you* need help, you will find it in these pages. The principles of healing used in the instances above were exactly those which you will find outlined here. If you need help, your reading this book is tantamount to asking for it.

### Now Your Defeats Can Become Victories

In all the examples above, note too that although fears, doubts, suspicions, and disbeliefs were strong, although evidence of impending failure was overwhelming, yet there was just enough hope, encouragement, and faith to lead those men and women to their "miracle." They finally changed the focus of their attention from the *acceptance of surrender* to the *inevitability of victory*. Acceptance of surrender, or at least the concentration upon its possibility has been the way of failure for ages. It has spawned the beggar, multiplied the pleader, and left the world strewn with the skeletons of starved hopes.

It is the way of the man who doubts God, and who never suspects why life did not bring him the happiness and health he wanted.

If you think you can't be helped, change the focus of your attention. Stop thinking so much of the failure of the self, of the inadequacy of others, the ineffectiveness of things. Return to a consciousness of union with the Source of all power. It is not the union of surrender, but of victory.

When you begin thinking of all the disastrous things that *could* happen to hurt you, quickly but quietly reject these things as having no reality for you. Instead, begin thinking of yourself as strong, healthy, successful. Practice the attitude that centers itself upon the *good* that can happen, not upon the possibility of *bad*.

Training in this is exactly like the training in anything else. Be consistent. Remember that you are really no different from anyone else. If anyone else can be helped, if anyone else can be healed, *so can you*.

### Your Healing Ideas for the Next 24 Hours

Write, type, or print the following thoughts on your three cards and use them as before, or simply mark this place in the book, and turn to it at the appropriate times.

EVENING

*My help is with me every moment of life. Tonight it will be with me while I sleep.*

*Tonight, while I sleep, my mind will be on only the presence of God, and all the joy, abundance, and health of that presence in me.*

*Whatever is wrong with me now is being healed even through this night, because nothing is hidden from, and nothing is impossible to God.*

MORNING

*I give thanks that last night I was in the presence of the Healing Power.*

*This morning I am awake to a conscious realization of that presence.*

*Last night I came closer to victory over illness. Today I shall continue that progress to my final victory.*

DAY

*Because I know that every thought is a prayer, and that every prayer infused with belief is an* answered *prayer, Today*

I think *only good, positive, healing* thoughts, *and*

*I shall allow myself to* believe *only in good positive, healing* things.

*Today I think as if my life depends upon it, because I know it does!*

# 3

## How Instantaneous Healing
## Can Be Available to
## You Anytime, Anywhere

It makes no difference whether one is

Kneeling on a prayer rug in the Near East,
Dancing around a fire in the jungle,
Sitting in a cathedral in France,
Entreating an intercessor at the Shrine of Lourdes,
Burning lamps on the steps of Chichicastenango,
Painting with sand in the land of the Navaho,
Spinning a prayer-wheel in Tibet, or
Receiving the laying-on-of-hands anywhere—

these are all ritualistic, unnecessary accoutrements of healing,
for healing needs no such decorations, embellishments or
elaborations.

At all times the Healing Power is within every person. It is
always ready, and it is *always the same*. It demands no ritual,
showmanship or fanfare to bring us the healing we seek.

Throughout his history man has invented thousands of ways
to increase his faith in something greater than he, to make it

easier for him to believe that this power has heard his plea, and will respond. He has rung bells, lit candles, learned litanies, danced, bathed, secluded himself in cloisters, forests, deserts, and pinnacles; he has tortured, starved, and denied himself— all of which served only to increase his own belief, for none of these things was necessary to activate the healing power itself.

Rituals and ceremonies practiced in an effort to call up the healing power have changed throughout cultures and time, but healing has remained always the same. Time and geography, instruments and actions are effective only as an elaboration of the essential fact that man believes, and that in his belief he has made the temple of his mind ready to receive the response of the healing power or presence within. We do not condemn anyone's constructive method of increasing his faith, but we warn against looking in the wrong direction for the healing power.

In recent years there has been a resurgence of interest in spiritual healing. Churches all over the world are returning to the concept of an Infinite Power which not only has the ability but also the inclination to heal. "Prayer," said Phillips Brooks, "is not the overcoming of God's reluctance, but the taking hold of God's willingness."

Frankly, the reader of this book is neither asked nor expected to desert either the acknowledgement of this power or the expectation and satisfaction of its healing touch.

### The Truth About Healing

Medical science, however, has made such giant strides in the last 40 years that many have worshipped *it* as the final answer. True, medical science has confronted bacteria and viruses on their own levels, and in many ways beaten them. Medical science continuously has developed the art of surgery, with its delicate incisions, manipulations, and excisions.

But physical correction and control do not possess, of themselves, the power to heal. For the most skillful operation to be successful, that Infinite power to heal must be present within the patient. For example, military science develops one weapon to combat or overcome another weapon developed by an enemy. The healing of the disease of war, however, lies not in developing greater weapons, but in the mental and spiritual development of the men who make them.

Every drug store has all kinds of patent medicines "for the relief of" this or that. "For the relief of symptoms due to...," their labels will proclaim, "for the relief of colds, neuralgia, congestion," "to stop pain," "to control coughs." You will note that nowhere is it said, "This medicine will *heal*."

The *Healing Power* cannot be found in a bottle, tube, jar, or needle.

It is not the sole province of the doctor, the minister, the medicine man, or the shaman.

It is not limited to operating tables, recovery rooms, sanitariums, or clinics.

It cannot be contained in a capsule or a powder.

When the doctor gives you a prescription, he does not include the promise that it will *heal* you. "This will *help* you," he says. "This will *relieve* you." "This will make you *feel* better." But he does *not* say, "This will *heal* you."

A sign over the entrance to a French hospital reads, "We treat the patient; God heals him."

In less theological language Voltaire paraphrased it, "The task of the doctor is to keep the patient happy while nature heals him."

### The Power of Harmony

A certain man paid $1,400 for an operation and the ensuing hospital expenses. He was cured of his difficulty, but he was not healed of the cause, for the cause was in his attitude toward life. Therefore, when he came home from the hospital the stage was still set for a recurrence of his illness, or for something else equally unwanted. He used a curative action, and only a portion of the healing power.

The ancient, and sometimes not-so-ancient theologians who insisted that we confess our sins in order to be "saved" were right. However, they twisted the purpose and method of this confession so that man always appeared innately sinful, unworthy of God's love, born in shame, and doomed to eke out a precarious existence through his debased and degraded humanity. On a premise that was laid down in spiritual truth, they erected a doctrinal structure that confused the issue, and made it appear that the "grace of God" was given or withheld by celestial judgment, not by every man himself according to both his understanding and practice of the principles of harmony and love.

Every negative and destructive thought, idea, or belief, no matter how justified it may be, no matter how documented by fact, supported by evidence, or sustained by illustration, is founded on a recognition that somewhere in this world there is disharmony. We must admit that there is disharmony. Look at the world situation today. Are we going to ignore it merely for the sake of entertaining no negative thoughts? Are we to say it just does not exist? Certainly not! This is the way of self-delusion, of self-hypnosis. Because it does exist, and because we can't ignore it, we seem impelled to believe in it to some extent, and to hold some ideas about it.

Nevertheless, as we think negatively, believe negatively, and hold negative ideas about something, we are, by just that much, separating ourselves from harmony itself, and by just that much, attracting the negative, inharmonious experiences into our lives.

### How to Clear the Way for Harmony

What, then, can we do?

First, we must recognize that we do have these problems of disharmony and negativity.

Second, we must do something about eliminating them, so that even justifiably, we need never again center our attention upon them. This is a big job for all of us, touching the economic, political, social, moral, mental, and spiritual patterns of the world.

On the personal, individual level, all this goes back to the old admonition: "Confess thy sins, and repent!" It does not mean to fall down in abject humiliation, and to cry out to God to forgive us and to grant us mercy. Rather, it means for us to stand up like men, to recognize where we have been weak or wrong, where we have been negative or in error (which is to "sin"), and to do somthing constructive about changing all this.

Then, when we begin to eliminate both the inharmonious thoughts and the reasons for them, we are beginning to "set the stage" for the healing process to begin.

The "confession" of our sins is, in our language, the inner, often secret admission that, in one thing or a hundred we have allowed ourselves to slip away from the laws of God, which simply means the laws of harmony. Whenever we have the slightest negative thought, we have become in that degree inharmonious, and, by just that much we remove ourselves from the protection of the Infinite.

Take note: It is not God who removes us from His harmony; we remove ourselves.

Whenever we clear our minds of negative and inharmonious attitudes and ideas, we begin using the power to heal, for it is waiting only for us to get ourselves out of the way. The so-called "confession" can be a frank, sincere discussion with a minister or practitioner, or it can be a completely private, personal revelation to one's self of what his problems and their causes are. It is done with the recognition and admission that God does not create the causes of our troubles and then punish us for succumbing to them, but that we create them, renew them, perpetuate them, and suffer for them.

Every effect has a cause. The causes of illness are not in

God's plan, but in man's mind. The purpose of effective prayer or treatment is to restate, or at least to imply our knowledge of this truth; to release our hold upon the inharmonious and the negative; to claim nothing but the right, the beautiful and the good; and thus set the stage to think or believe nothing that will block this healing power. The purpose of prayer, in other words, as Phillips Brooks pointed out, is not to overcome God's reluctance, but to take hold of God's willingness.

### How to Achieve a Clean Mind for a Sound Body

Now, let's see how it works. Let's assume we are ill, sick, disease-ridden. Disharmony rules our body. We have tried so many things—drugs, operations, psychology, psychiatry, hypnotism, physical therapy, meditation, and prayer. Why can we not find the answer? Why are we still sick and discouraged? Why are we told that we are "incurable"? Hasn't it been said that to God all things are possible? Then why can't we find our healing?

In the first place, we have looked for the *relief*, and failed to believe in the *healing*. We may have supposed that we needed something different, some new innovation, some wonder-drug, without realizing that true healing is always the same.

Perhaps we have struggled to get rid of the effect, but done nothing to eliminate the cause. If a man takes pills to reduce his high blood pressure, and does nothing about the high pressure life he is living and thinking, he merely suppresses the effect; he has not eliminated the cause. He has found a "cure," or relief, but he has not been healed. The "time-bomb" is still ticking away in his system. If we cut our finger, we wash the wound in order to cleanse it of dirt and poisons so that the healing can take place unimpeded and without contamination. But when more serious wounds of the body and of life are suffered, we should be aware that this is a warning of even more serious poisons within the mind. Then we must cleanse the mind of its poisons so that healing here, too, can take place unimpeded and without contamination. It is as important to cleanse the mind of its mental poisons, as it is to cleanse the finger of its physical ones. Only then can we be sure we have truly begun to use the power to heal.

In our search for healing, we may say we have tried prayer. Why, then, hadn't the prayer been answered? Its failure could be due not to what it included, but to what it excluded. Perhaps it included the recognition of God and the Infinite Power, a statement of certain desires and needs, a claim upon those desires, the satisfaction of those needs, and an evidence of faith. All are excellent and essential elements of treatment (prayer). But what is missing? Why are we not freed of our illnesses? Because we have neither acknowledged nor made any effort whatsoever to remove the causes of our illness. Somewhere we have allowed ourselves to fall out of harmony with some part of our world. Somewhere, justified or not, we have allowed the poisons of negative ideas, beliefs, and emotions to insinuate themselves into our minds, and we have thus impeded and contaminated the healing power. Therefore, the treatment (or the prayer) should include the theologian's so-called "confession of sin" with, however, a different understanding of what it means and the purpose for which it has been included. The actual, conscious rejection of these sins or errors of consciousness must follow, plus the conviction that we can and will go and sin no more.

## Why "Relief" Only Avoids Healing Power

You are aware that this does not propose merely the emotional "relief" sought by those who want to be free of their pains yet hang on to their errors. Such relief is the way of the bottle and the pill, the needle and the knife. These may supplement, at times, but they will never supplant the healing power.

That power is always ready, waiting for us to set the stage. If we want the body to be cleansed of its ills, we must first cleanse the mind.

This is not an easy verdict for those who are hoping for a "miracle" simply by beseeching God, and demonstrating to Him how faithful they are. It is not an easy verdict for those who practice all the accoutrements of healing, but prefer to forget what must occur in the temple of the mind. But this book does not teach the easy way of "relief." We are not perfect, yet we must strive for perfection. Furthermore, our failure to achieve perfection must not be allowed to upset us, for even this is a demonstration of our imperfection. We cannot persist in our imperfect attitudes and ideas, and expect to get more than a temporary "relief," or, at the most, an imperfect healing.

### Eliminate the Negative

Do you hate your neighbor?

Do you become irritated by false claims?

Do you get upset when you wait overlong in a restaurant—annoyed at those who can't make up their minds—angry at the driver in front of you who causes you to miss a signal—worried by a delay in your plans—afraid of what could happen tomorrow?

Do you carry a grudge against someone who deliberately tried to be disagreeable and mean?

Do you feel guilty about what happened in the past—bitter about dreams that were shattered—suspicious of someone in the office trying to double-cross you?

Are you jealous of someone doing better than you—outraged at some of the lies told about you?

You could be or do all these things, and perhaps be found justified in at least half of them. Yes, perhaps you could. But you *dare* not; you *must* not; and, if you follow the suggestions in this book, you *will* not. For by just that much you place your-self out of harmony with God's laws, and by just that much will you be missing their protection when you need it most.

If you want true and permanent healing, you must be willing to release all negative and destructive ideas, even while you are working to remove their justification, for to heal the wounds in the bodies of this world, we must first cleanse its minds.

This is the truth from which generations have fled, seeking an easier way for the miracle to touch their inflamed and pain-wracked flesh. But there is no easier way. We offer no panaceas that bypass the healed mind. We hold out no shortcuts to the heaven of health that do not go through the process of eliminating the destructive idea.

Whenever we treat for anyone anywhere in the world, we include (in thought if not in actual words) the expression of our belief in their intention to eliminate all destructive causes in mind, and a subsequent conviction that it is done. Even without this, healing can and does take place through faith alone. Too often, however, it is only temporary, a fading cure, a quick relief, while the mental stage is still set for a recurrence of the illness or for another equally troublesome condition.

Therefore, if we want our bodies to be temples of strength and wholeness, we must cast out those attitudes and beliefs which are negative and unwholesome, for whether we know it, admit it, or believe it, inevitably they reflect themselves in an unwholesome body. This has been the law of healing since the first wound of body and mind was sealed up and made whole. This is one of the reasons why true healing is always the same. It is your assurance that if the power is present (which it is), and you meet the conditions as outlined in this book (which you will), the wonderful experience of healing will be yours.

The following healing ideas are to be used from tonight to tomorrow night. Remember that lip service is not enough. Truly accept these ideas and make them a part of your beliefs.

EVENING

> This bed of mine is a healing shrine tonight because the heal-
> ing power is here.
>
> Tonight I release all hatreds, grudges, jealousies, suspicions,
> irritations, worries, fears, and anger. I cannot afford them.
> Therefore, I give them no place in my waking or sleeping
> hours.
>
> Tonight I unite myself with Harmony. Tonight my dreams
> are free of conflict, and my mind is centered on peace.

MORNING

> I give thanks for last night. It brought me closer to harmony
> with myself and with my world.
>
> Through this past night I have become bigger than the de-
> structive habits, beliefs, and emotions I might have had
> yesterday.
>
> Today will be a discovery—I shall find new ways to express
> the Harmony within me.

DAY

> Today no one can hurt me because I refuse to believe in
> being hurt.
>
> Today I remain above anything and everything that tries to
> make me angry, jealous, irritable, or afraid.
>
> Today I see only the pleasant side of life because that is
> what I am looking for.
>
> Today the same healing that has come to others waits for me.
>
> Today I am in harmony with all of life.

# 4

## Why You Must Want to Get Well More Than You Want to Remain Ill

One of the most explosive questions one can ask those who are trying everything they can think of to get well is this:

"Do you want to get well more than you want to remain ill?"

It is a strange sort of question, to be sure, one that sometimes causes a violent reaction from the person asked.

"Do you mean you think I don't *want* to get well?"

Then he will itemize the money he has spent, the time he has lost, the suffering he has undergone. He will think it preposterous that there could be the slightest doubt that he truly wants to get well.

Consciously, of course, he does want to get well. But what subconscious reasons does he have for remaining ill? What hidden motives, what secret needs demand his suffering, or block his healing? In these he will find the answers to his illness.

There are thousands, perhaps hundreds of thousands of men and women suffering today who *could* get well, but who won't, because somewhere in life they are accepting—hidden though it may be—an apparent compensation for illness that to them is too good to exchange for health. There is a certain value received in return for their pain, and although the pain is at times almost unbearable, it is even more unbearable to think of giving up whatever it brings them.

There are additional thousands who take pride in their illnesses. "My arthritis," they will say, actually claiming as theirs that which, at the same time, they claim they do not want—"my ulcers," "my headaches," "my bad liver," "my weak heart," "my sensitive stomach." They will discuss their aches and pains at the slightest provocation, and often if the provocation is not there they will make one. Many of those who glory in their illness would vehemently dispute the idea that they would rather be ill than well. It is these who remain ill, because they do not have the courage to ask themselves that question, "Do I really want to get well more than I want to remain ill?"

Millions of dollars are spent annually in the useless pursuit of healing. Sometimes family budgets are drained when one of the family members outwardly seeks to be healed, and inwardly wants to hang on to his illness. This pursuit of health then becomes one of the greatest hoaxes a person can play upon his family and himself.

When we begin searching for ways to get well, to overcome some chronic or recurrent illness, we must first face the honest answer to this:

> "Is there any hidden reason for me to remain ill? Is there some subconscious motivation that drew this illness to me and that makes it convenient or advisable to keep it? What am I getting as a result of this illness that I would lose if I were to get well?"

These may be startling questions, but they are of the utmost importance to anyone seeking an instantaneous healing.

For those who are puzzled by some chronic or recurrent illness, here are some additional, and more pointed, questions. They are followed by examples of those who might have answered "Yes."

1. *Does illness give you a sense of power over those who are concerned with you, or who must take care of you?*

Philip Argenta was a timid boy who felt inadequate in the presence of others his own age, and rejected by his elders. He wanted to be loved. He wanted attention. He believed he was the object of neither. As he grew older he became afraid to face the world as his older brothers and sisters had done. He had nothing to offer.

His parents were urging him to find some kind of work he wanted to follow. He felt they were pushing him out when he wasn't ready to go. He was angry at them for wanting to get rid of him. But every day he went looking for a job.

One morning he couldn't get out of bed. He couldn't explain what it was he felt—he was just too weak. A day or two later, however, he went out, once more looking for work. Before noon he collapsed and had to be brought home in an ambulance. That was the last time he ever left the house. His parents take care of him now. Their boy has some mysterious ailment that the doctors can't seem to cure.

Philip Argenta at last has achieved dominance in his family. Those who neglected him are now deeply concerned over every rise and fall of his temperature. Their world revolves around his day-to-day condition. His brothers and sisters come to see him. He has attention he never received before. He wouldn't give it all up for the world, or at least for the health that would take it all away and make him go back out into that world again to be forgotten and neglected, responsible for himself.

Although his father and mother spend a great amount of money for his doctors, and although the others in the family help out now and then, even when it works a hardship on them, Philip Argenta doesn't want to get well.

2. *Does illness enable you to escape from an unwanted or un-*
   *desirable duty, task, or responsibility?*

Alan Demming found himself in a business he detested. It
was a business in which he was "successful"—that is, he made
money. He had built his way of life on that success, and that
way of life depended upon his sticking to the job. His wife had
her own new car; his two children were in an expensive college;
his future was mortgaged to the last possible extent of his
projected income.

Alan Demming was trapped. Every day that he opened the
door to his office, he gritted his teeth and cursed silently. He
couldn't quit. It wasn't the money alone. What would he say
to his wife, his friends, his business associates? What excuse
would he use for throwing it all over? He would look foolish.
Everyone would call him crazy. Nobody did things like that.
There just didn't seem to be any way out.

Then one day Alan Demming had a heart attack. It wasn't
enough to incapacitate him, but the doctor told him he'd have
to stop all his hard work. Yes, it would mean giving up the
business, or turning it over to someone else. If not, the doctor
told him, a severe attack might come. It could be fatal.

Alan Demming gave all the indications of a man crushed
under the blow. For a while his condition was critical. No one
criticized him now for closing the business and getting out with
the least possible loss. After all, he had to be careful.

His "condition" continued until well after the last vestige
of the business had disappeared, and there was no possibility of
his going back into it. Gradually, after that, he became well.
Today he is not so successful financially, but he is working at
something he likes. He has never been so well. He wants to be
well now, but when he was ill, he wanted to be ill.

Susan Ekhart is a clerk-typist. Her job entails much walking
between offices. It is a good job and pays well, but Susan
resents having to work. She thinks she should be married—that

a man should be taking care of her. But her constant resentment and negativity have soured her personality. She does not attract men.

When she gets to the point where her resentment reaches hysterical proportions, her foot swells, gets inflamed, and pains her so that she cannot stand on it. Because the doctor has no remedy for her emotions, all he can do is to advise her to go home and stay off the foot until it gets well. This she does gladly. Only when her sick-leave runs out and there is no alternative except returning to work, does the swelling subside and the pain end.

Susan Ekhart does not really want to be sick, she does not want her foot to be sore, but her escape-motive is stronger than her work-motive. Subconsciously she makes the foot become painful and swollen as her only way out. When her sick-leave builds up again, she will want to be ill more than she wants to be well because it will be the only way she can stay home from the office and get paid for it.

### 3. *Is your illness your way of punishing someone?*

The persons we punish through our own illness almost always are loved ones. They are the only ones whose interest can be counted upon to be perpetuated through our long suffering. And of course, if they are average men and women (or children), they suffer along with us.

Mrs. Ralph Claydell was a career woman. Her husband was an analyst in a stock and bond house. His hours were rather regular. She was busy most of the time attending meetings, conferences, and conventions. Mr. Claydell found it convenient to spend a considerable amount of time with some of his company's women customers. Soon it became evident that he was happy with his wife's many absences. Shortly thereafter it also became evident to his wife. She was furious. She would have divorced him immediately, but their religion frowned upon such action. She hated him.

She developed a severe case of colitis, followed by a dangerous kidney infection. She was rushed to the hospital. For a time it was thought that she wouldn't live. But she did. The operation and the subsequent hospitalization took almost all of Mr. Claydell's savings. He was forced to bring her home, but he did not have the income to provide her with adequate care. It was up to him to be with her at every possible moment. He had neither the time nor the money now to follow his old pursuits. Mrs. Claydell suffered for the next twelve years, never getting quite well enough to be on her own. By necessity, Mr. Claydell was her constant companion. Neither one enjoyed the company of the other, but through her illness, Mrs. Claydell enjoyed a secret happiness in punishing her husband for his indiscretions.

Another woman, Mrs. Bretsch, suffered a fall immediately after learning that her husband sold some property without her knowledge. She had signed a paper once without realizing that she had signed away to him all her right, title, and interest in the property. The fall had so injured her back that she became paralyzed. He had to push her everywhere, and care for her every need. He was an active, dynamic person, and this way of life was completely out of character for him. In his own words, he was "nursemaid to a hopeless invalid."

I had an opportunity to talk with this woman. I suspected that there was a hidden motive in her paralysis, and that actually there was no physiological reason for her paralysis. I suggested to her that perhaps this was her subconscious way of punishing him for his mistakes. She protested vehemently. It was ridiculous of me even to think of such a thing, let alone suspect it! She refused to see me again.

Five years later I met her at a concert. She was walking easily. She looked well. I commented upon her recovery. "Yes," she said, and she gave me a half-smile, "I got well last year. I thought he had suffered enough." With that she walked away, and I have never seen her again.

4. *Is illness your way of punishing yourself for some sense of
   personal guilt?*

Jack Sebastian committed a minor crime when he was seven-
teen. No one ever found out. He was considered by everyone
a "good" boy. He had never had any intention of committing
the crime in the first place, and his conscience bothered him
from the moment it happened. He was afraid to tell anyone.
He kept the secret within himself. But almost every night he
dreamed about it. He felt that someone's life had been ruined
because of it. He would never be able to repay for what he had
done.

Gradually, as Jack grew older, those who would have been
shocked, or hurt, or somehow involved with him because of his
crime moved away, or died. Finally, there was no one who
would ever find out. His secret was a secret forever.

But unfortunately it was not a secret from Jack. There was
no one to punish him. Even God had somehow overlooked him.
In his deep and abiding sense of guilt, there was only one who
could punish him—himself. Of course he did not reason this out.
He would have objected and denied it if it had been pointed
out to him at the time. But now only Jack was in a position to
render judgment and visit punishment upon himself.

He developed severe pains throughout his stomach and back.
No amount of treatment could ease them. He walked bent over.
He was never able to do much work. He was lonely, but found
no one who wanted to share his life. He offered only the possibility of a long future of suffering and hardship. He would have
given almost anything to be well, but there was the self-created
need for punishment that would not let him get well. He felt
he deserved punishment more than he deserved happiness and
health.

Jack came to see me one day on a matter of business. What
he revealed to me made me begin to question him about his
private, personal life. He said very little until about the fifth

time he came, when he told me the whole story in complete detail. What he did not say (because he was not consciously aware of it) was that because there was no one else to punish him, he had been punishing himself.

I told him that the young man who had committed that crime of years ago no longer existed. That the memory which he carried was the memory of an act committed by someone who was now a stranger to him, and that I was as sure as he was that today the commission of such an act would be completely and irrevocably foreign to his nature. He agreed.

"Why, then," I asked him, "is the man you are today suffering for the act of that young man of years ago? Why are you punishing him? Why don't you forgive him, release him, and let him go? You made a mistake. But is that any reason to bind your life to that mistake? You are just as much in error right now, re-living that awful night, as you were in living it then. You have punished yourself enough. I think it is time now to remember the words of Jesus: 'Go, and sin no more.' Which means as well—forget the past, and make the present what you have the power to make it."

Jack Sebastian did just that. His healing was instantaneous. The only reason for his sickness had disappeared in a moment of revelation and clarity. The cause was gone, and so was the effect.

The instances in which illness is found to be a substitute for something else that seems unattainable are far more numerous than most of us suspect. What is missing in the life which suffers pain?

Illness has many values to sick, immature minds. Whereas health would:

    Rob them of certain power,
    Force them to face responsibility,
    Deny them the sympathy they crave, or
    Enlarge their already painful sense of guilt—
illness allows them to avoid such consequences.

If you want to get well with only 49% of your being, and reserve 51% for a desire to remain ill, all the other secrets of healing will be of little use. The failure to discover this secret is responsible for the almost complete puzzlement, frustration, and discouragement of those whose loved ones, for instance, remain ill and pain-wracked for no apparent reason, and in spite of the best and most expensive medical care and attention possible.

### The Truth That Can Make You Whole

The following truths are for all those who may suspect that their illness has some "value" motive. They are also good for anyone else who must deal with the recurrently or chronically ill.

1. *Every problem has a creative solution. Nothing is truly hopeless.*

The mind is a magnet which attracts experiences to match what it loves, fears, or steadily expects. That upon which it centers its attention is that which begins to gravitate toward it. The attention must be turned from the undesirable to the desirable, from the destructive or negative aspects of our situation to the constructive and positive ones.

The irritating part of anything—a job, another person, a situation, a condition—is not in the job, person, situation, or condition, but in our *reaction* to these things. Nothing possesses resentment or irritation of itself. We endow it with such qualities by our *reaction* to it.

2. *We do not need to accept substitutes in life.*

We so often have made the mistake of thinking that specific *things* are necessary to satisfy our desires, when it is only a *condition* that we seek to gain through those things. You may think that it is a *specific thing* that will make you happy. Analyze your desire. What you really want is the achievement of a certain *condition.*

For instance, a man says, "I must have that woman for mine. No one else will satisfy me."

What he does not realize is that this specific woman, while made the object of his desire, becomes that object *only* because, through her, he expects to satisfy a more basic desire for love, attention, affection, sex. The satisfaction of this condition *may* come through this specific woman, but the desire for this woman is secondary to the desire for the achievement of a *condition.*

If finally he marries this woman, then he has accepted her as the appropriate agent or channel *through* which he will be able to satisfy the condition he desires.

Another man says, "I want ten thousand dollars." More than likely it is not the ten thousand dollars he wants, but the *condition* that such an amount of money will make possible.

Too often we substitute the *way-point* for the *destination.* We must find what our destination (our true goal) is and begin concentrating on *that.*

3. *Illness is man's poorest substitute for a condition he feels he cannot reach, and the most damaging method of escape from something he does not want.*

Know that you *can* achieve the conditions you want, and that you have the right openly to reject any other condition you do not want without the subterfuge of illness.

4. *To punish the body for some failure of the spirit is the mark of the sick, immature mind.*

"It just makes me sick!" is a common expression. It is the confession of immaturity, the admission of an inability to manage one's own thoughts, and to discipline one's own emotions.

5. *Punishment by illness (whether that punishment is directed toward others or toward ourselves) disputes and denies the ancient power of forgiveness.*

Whatever happened in the past, through us or to us, must be left in the past. It must not be dragged into the present by either a vengeful or a self-righteous mind.

THEREFORE:

*Refuse* to accept illness as the answer to *any* unsolved problem.

*Refuse* to make illness a weapon, an excuse, a camouflage, or a substitute for *anything*.

*Admit* that the so-called benefits of illness are far less compatible with life than the benefits of health.

Right now, *reject* every conscious and subconscious reason for hanging on to an illness because it offers some "value" to your life.

*Declare* that from this moment on you are not going to delude yourself into believing that illness brings you *anything* that you cannot get more easily, effortlessly, and happily through health.

Face yourself squarely, and ask yourself, "Am I 49% in favor of getting well, but 51% in favor of being sick?" That difference of 2% may be the difference between chronic illness and your INSTANTANEOUS HEALING.

YOU MUST WANT TO GET WELL MORE THAN YOU WANT TO REMAIN ILL!

Now—*put these healing ideas into ACTION:*

•··•··•··•··•··•··•··•··•··•··•··•··•··•··•··•··•··•··•··•··•··•··•··•··•··•··•··•··•··•··•··•··•·

EVENING

*Tonight I release my illness. It is of no use to me.*

*Tonight I know that every need I have can be and will be satisfied, not through my illness, but through my health.*

*I truly want to get well.*

•··•··•··•··•··•··•··•··•··•··•··•··•··•··•··•··•··•··•··•··•··•··•··•··•··•··•··•··•··•··•··•··•·

MORNING

*This morning I look forward to every challenge facing me during this day. I do not want to "escape" anything.*

*For every job, problem, or responsibility I can call upon an inner strength that will be mine when I need it.*

*I truly want to get well.*

DAY

*All sense of punishment—for myself or others—is gone. There is never any need for any punishment through my illness. I will not be ill to get revenge, to hurt someone else, or to punish myself.*

*I do not need to accept substitutes for the health and happiness I want.*

*I truly want to get well—and I am getting well.*

# 5

## How to Prepare for
## the Healing You Want

Pressures surround us on every side. We may not give them
our conscious attention, but too often we allow them to affect
us subconsciously. When those subconscious reactions are sustained over a long period of time, eventually we may come to
a conscious awareness that we are close to a breaking point.
When finally we realize that our nerves are shaking, that we
are close to breaking down, that our body is reflecting the un-
certainty, confusion, and overload we are feeling in mind, we
desperately begin searching for something to save us, to rescue
us from a terrible sense of disaster. We think of escape, of quit-
ting everything. Some of us have a nervous breakdown in order
not to break down in our work. We grasp at substitutes, at
panaceas, at almost anything that offers even a slight hope in
a critical situation.

But the time to begin looking for something to avoid the
breakdowns in life is not when those breakdowns are imminent,
when we already have allowed ourselves to get to the point
where we are afraid it is too late. The time to begin is when

life is going along very well, when we have our straight-thinking, our stability and our health. The man who is prepared to avoid the breakdowns of life is the man who will not have to experience them.

When business breaks down, when nerves "break down," when confidence, faith, happiness, security, and well-being break down, when all the wonderful things of life begin cracking up, it is then that we need to know what to do, how to act, what to think to avert the tragedy that seems just around the corner. It is then that we need to begin preparing ourselves for the moment of victory over such threats and conditions, for that instant when we can say, "I am well!"

At some time or other almost everyone has reached that point of intensity where faith obliterates the merely human and reveals only the divine; where fear, consciousness of the problem, and realization of possible failure all disappear in a moment of spiritual inspiration. These are the times when prayer suddenly is answered, when, almost without notice, the problem is a problem no more.

Unfortunately, however, such moments are rare. So the problem drags on, treatment fails, and discouragement sets in. Thus the world prays, often with only a forlorn hope. And even before the prayer, the prayer is already doomed.

It is then that we must discover the secret that healing cannot be achieved without some kind of preparation. Whether that preparation takes place in the mind of the one seeking the healing, or in the mind of the one who is called in to do some spiritual treatment for that healing, is not important, but it must take place in one or the other.

This book is your preparation for the potential emergency of illness and the demand for its healing. More than that, it is your preparation for *health,* for if one follows the principles explained here, the crisis of illness will not occur.

## The Result of Preparation

Here are some instances where healing took place because the one asking for help was ready to receive it, and the one asked for help was prepared to give it.

A woman writes to me that her doctor ordered her to the hospital for an operation. She asked for more time to think about it, and called our office for treatment. Following this, she requested new X-rays. The X-rays now showed nothing to be wrong. There was no operation.

One treatment request told of a child of three whose blood vessels were breaking down. It was in the hospital facing a "last resort" operation. The man requesting the treatment explained that the doctors had little hope or expectation of help from the operation. Despite their disbelief, however, "recovery was rapid and complete."

In his letter of thanks the man wrote:

> It is a wonderful thing to be able to accept the truth that treatment is answered so fully and completely. We have had so many demonstrations that we are able to accept it as the norm for us. I can remember when I would have said: "It was nice of them to pray for her, but they had to operate anyway." It is strange indeed that people will pray to achieve an end, and when it is realized, will promptly pick apart the means by which it was achieved.

After a telephone call for treatment made by a friend at the request of the woman involved, there was an immediate release from pain, and ease of delivery in childbirth.

From another woman's written report:

> At 4:00 P.M. today the problem you treated for looked hopeless. At 4:30 P.M. it was answered in a most unexpected way.

Another letter reads:

> A couple of weeks ago I had a very bad nasal hemor-
> rhage. I had tried for a couple of days to treat myself,
> but I guess my own fear prevented it. However, within a
> few moments after calling you for help the bleeding
> stopped. Please accept my heartfelt thanks.

### The "Middle-Man" and His Purpose

The cases noted above are typical of so many others in my
personal files from such men and women who asked for help
for themselves. It should be pointed out also, however, that
instantaneous healings are possible even when the one who is
ill is unaware of the treatment taking place. The receptivity
is not, at the moment, in the mind of the one who is ill, but in
the mind of the one who is doing the treating. He is somewhat
of a "middle-man," whose purpose is to supply the faith that
may be missing in the mind of the one who is ill. He acts as the
"distributing agent" for the Healing Power. It is his knowledge
of the healing art which he applies to the illness of another.

One report reads:

> For three days I had suffered from severe cold and
> laryngitis. On Thursday night, without my knowledge,
> treatment was requested for me. The remarkable thing
> about this entire experience was the fact that the heal-
> ing was instantaneous, and it occurred at approximately
> 9:00 P.M., which is about the time you and your group
> join in the treatment period.

This report concerned a request for treatment from a friend.
The request was handed to me for our treatment during one of
our regular Thursday evening meetings. At the close of the
meetings we take each request and give it our attention and
treatment based entirely upon our knowledge of the principles
outlined in this book. In this case the communication between
mind and Mind was perfect, and healing took place. It must

also be pointed out, however, that in order for this person to *remain* healed, he must eliminate the *causes* of his illness. We shall deal with this phase of healing in later chapters.

### When the "Middle-Man" Is Unnecessary

Healings like those above do occur, and they occur regularly. But the surest, soundest method of healing is for the person who needs to be healed to begin his *own* preparation, so that he need depend upon no one but himself when the time for healing arrives.

A young man and his wife had tried unsuccessfully for four years to have a baby. Instead, there were three miscarriages. They began studying and applying the principles explained here. They read everything I would give them. Their entire attitude changed. They corrected errors of thinking. They found their faith lifting. They began to believe in a strong, healthy, beautiful child. In other words, they *prepared* for what they wanted.

From the mother's letter came these words:

> Both my husband and I wish to extend our thanks to God, and in so doing wish to thank you for the wonderful work you did for us. If it hadn't been for the things you taught us, we know we wouldn't have the wonderful little daughter born to us last August 11th. I never forgot the thoughts you gave us. We are so thankful.

Preparation, and the application of that preparation, was one of the secrets of this couple's healing.

Such preparation was necessary even to one who already had prepared herself in another way.

"I had been trained in the modern attitude therapy which borders closely upon what you teach," wrote Miss L. G. of a certain well-known hospital clinic, "and have watched psychosomatic medicine grow from a heretic whisper to a recognizable roar in the medical profession.

"I still felt," she continued, "that there was a badly missing answer that we were not providing our patients. After all we could do for them, and they went out of the hospital well and happy, soon we had to take them back, in worse condition than the time before because the fundamental cure was not there."

It was at this time she discovered our work.

"I have now been studying your methods and teaching for the past two years, and have found many answers that I have been looking for for many years for myself, my profession and my friends. I have found in your methods and teaching the missing dimension that frustrated me so as a therapist working in psychiatric situations. In fact, I found you and your work just in time to prevent a serious nervous breakdown of my own, and have been enabled to work my way through many depths of hostilities and insecurities to a sense of balance, freedom and understanding."

This woman met her own health crisis because, while preparing herself through our work to meet the crises of others, she had also prepared for her own. The timely application of these principles saved her from serious physical and emotional breakdown.

### Healing Is More Than Physical

We begin to see that behind every authentic healing there is preparation. Often this preparation must overcome long years of training in reverse. Nor is healing limited only to the physical levels of life. More often than not it is the mental, emotional, and spiritual being which needs healing, with the realization of course that continued illness of this level will lead to corresponding illnesses on the physical one.

The pleasure of receiving such a letter as the following one is great, but not so great as satisfaction at seeing the principles which *you* are receiving through this book put to such effective use.

The writer explained that her early training had been in a family that had practiced stiff reserve and a suspicion of almost all sentiment and emotion. The impression such training had left with her had all but ruined her marriage, and had caused her nothing but suffering.

She wrote:

> Thanks to your teaching the tables are turning. We are all much happier, and learning to say and show what we feel. In the beginning it was only an exchange between me and the children, but it spreads.
>
> I could write volumes, but it would only be a repetition of a deeply felt and crudely expressed appreciation for the opportunity to learn what you teach. And how does one go about saying such things? They sound maudlin. One assumes that such things go without saying.
>
> The thing is, by the time one accomplishes a miracle, it takes on the appearance of only the norm, and no more than to be expected. So one is left with the feeling that in your position you must see and hear of even greater ones happening every day. Yet, I have been humbly grateful for the way you get things across so that we can understand what you are getting at. It certainly must be understood to be used.
>
> When I look back about five years (when I started studying with you), my life has been one miracle after another. I didn't even know living could be like this. And I'm only just beginning.
>
> I've come from the verge of divorce to an exceptionally happy marriage; from the brink of a nervous breakdown to greater emotional stability than I knew existed in a mere human.
>
> All I can say is, "Thank you." Not only for myself, but for my children. For them it could have been pure hell. Now they are happy (and slightly spoiled) kids, who have every chance to become good, backbone-of-the-community adults. I've come a long way!

"Back from the verge of divorce." "Back from the brink of a nervous breakdown." "Back from the prospect that this was the end." The stories of lives saved, of happiness restored, of sanity preserved are endless from those who have had the wisdom to *prepare*.

### "The Foolish Despise Wisdom and Instruction"

The unknown writer of the opening lines of the Biblical anthology known as Proverbs knew the value of preparation centuries ago:

> To know wisdom and instruction;
> To discern the words of understanding;
> To receive instruction in wise dealing,
> In righteousness and judgement and equity;
> To give subtlety to the simple,
> To the young man knowledge and discretion:
> That the wise man may hear, and increase in learning;
> And that the man of understanding
> May attain unto sound counsels:
> To understand a proverb, and a figure;
> The words of the wise, and their dark sayings.
>
> The fear of the Lord is the beginning of knowledge,
> But the foolish despise wisdom and instruction.[1]

### How to Use the Four Key Counsels When Preparing

To add to the preparation for healing and health which you have been making, consider the "sound counsels" contained in the following suggestions:

1. *Be prepared for what you want by thinking of it as inevitable.*

Keep telling yourself that you cannot fail. Build an attitude of expectancy.

---

[1] Proverbs 1:2-7.

Forget precedent, history, prophecy. If you start recounting to yourself all the reasons why you could fail, and the obstacles that could fall in your way, the time for the miracle is already past.

You need a state of mind in which there is neither room nor time for failure.

The newspapers recently carried the story of a 126-pound woman who lifted a 3600-pound station-wagon. Impossible? It would have been if she had stopped to reason with herself about it. But she did not stop. First, there was a strong motive for her sudden action. Her son was pinned beneath the station-wagon. Second, she did not have time or take time to tell herself that lifting that tremendous load was impossible. There was only one dominant fact—the station-wagon *had* to be lifted, and she was there to do it. Third, it was absolutely the *only* thing to which, at the moment, she gave her attention. Everything else was blotted out. Nothing else, at that precise point, interfered with her concentration on the job at hand.

This nationally-publicized incident recalled to mind an experience of my own. Walking along a street one day I saw smoke coming from an old frame house. It seemed to be on fire. At that instant I saw a big, upright piano come rolling out of the house onto the front porch. It practically careened out the front door. After it came a woman, a single, diminutive, desperate woman. She was pushing that piano alone. The fire proved to be a small one and was soon extinguished. It was time to move the piano back into the house. I volunteered to help the woman. Before we were able to get the piano back where it belonged, we needed the woman, myself, two other men, and a boy.

## What Makes the Difference Between Success and Failure?

What was the difference between the woman's individual success, and our subsequent individual failure? What made a group effort necessary where an individual effort had been enough before? *The difference was preparation.* The woman was instantly prepared for her task by eliminating every idea of failure, accepting only the inevitability of doing what she had to do, and pin-pointing her attention on the job at hand.

When the crisis had passed, however, she realized how big and heavy that old piano really was. Now she could stop to think about the obstacles, the impossibility of moving it inside again by herself. Now she could see why she couldn't do it. Once again reason took command. She was joined by one who also could see the difficulty, if not the impossibility of the task. Finally, four minds, which were well aware of the weight and clumsiness of the piano, were needed to move the necessary muscles into effective action. We had prepared ourselves with a belief in our own limitations, and the limitations, of course, bound us to our beliefs.

## Do Not Hang on to Your Illness

Any hanging on to a problem, through a realization of how serious it is, how seldom it is ever healed, or by any claim upon it as "yours," will delay the healing, prevent its instant consummation, or block it completely.

Any acknowledgement of the reality of the condition creating the illness or the problem gives power to the condition, and prolongs the problem.

Only the final, perfect state to be desired must be visualized and accepted. You must see through the worldly "realities" into the spiritual realities. Without doubt or hesitation you must claim what you want to be the truth about you and your condition. Claim health. Do not claim the illness.

If you allow yourself to be influenced by "reason," by the evidence of your senses, which tell you of the worldly seriousness of your illness—

If you lose yourself in medical history or terminology—

If you are discouraged by your past failures at healing—or the history of other failures with difficulties like yours—

If you are looking for the opinions and judgments of your friends—

Then you have slipped back into the world of fear and hopelessness. You have invited the experience of failure. You have lost a precious grip on the world of faith and inevitability. You have lost—for the time at least—your chance for success. Your preparation for healing has been too little. *It has been overcome by your preparation for illness.*

2. *Be prepared* now *for what you want* now.

Live in the expectancy of that which you want happening *today.*

Too many men and women are intimidated by time. They gaze hopefully, or doubtfully into the future. They are surrounded by those who warn them, "You've got a long time to wait."

But whatever the mechanical, arbitrary, or inherent time-element involved in what you want, no matter how long you are told it takes a certain disease or illness to be healed, refuse to live in the consciousness of that time. Rather, *live in the consciousness of the desire, the dream, the healing already having been achieved and fulfilled.*

Remember, however, it is one thing to affirm your good, and another to be receptive to your ills. Usually an affirmation is based only on desire, while receptivity is founded principally on belief. When belief and desire are in conflict, *belief always wins.*

3. *Give your whole self to the idea of the healing you desire.*

Limited giving of the self (of the mind) creates limited receiving. When you turn to sport, to work, to study, or to prayer, *practice the undivided mind.* This is the pin-point concentration employed by the woman who lifted the station-wagon.

Simply to hope, to wish, to dream, to recognize only the need, is limited giving of the mind. Accepting substitutes, half-way measures, or "relief" is also limited giving. The mind must be dedicated to the concept of healing, not to the prospect of illness.

4. *Ask yourself the question: "How much do I believe in the healing I want?" Limited believing also means limited receiving.*

Walter Davis was a world-champion high-jumper. But he would never have become that world-champion without a belief that he would, for when Davis was eight years old his legs crumpled with polio. He was told he would never walk again. A visitor convinced him that if he would believe in the help of God to make it possible, he would walk again and he would not have to remain a cripple all his life. He and his mother talked it over. Together they began "seeing" him as a strong, healthy, athletic young man. In his imagination he began high-jumping. He saw himself sailing easily and effortlessly over the bar. The mental image became stronger each week. *This was his period of preparation.* He began exercising a little each day. He increased it as he grew stronger.

Walter Davis became well enough to marry, and then it was his wife who dreamed, imagined, and believed with him. Daily he developed his leg-power, but his wife pointed out that he also daily developed the power of his belief.

It is enough to say that Walter Davis made the United States Olympic team, and in the high-jump set his world-record. To others it was "unbelievable," "incredible." To Walter Davis it was completely believable, and therefore inevitable.

When you have the need or desire to be healed, *believe in it,* and believe in it for *you.*

### We Prepare for Instantaneous Illness— Why Not for Instantaneous Healing?

A certain man has a heart-attack. It comes upon him in the midst of work, during a quiet hour at home, on a trip, or anywhere. One moment he is well, happy, busy, unconcerned. The next he is struck down, incapacitated. Soon he could be dead.

It was unexpected. It was sudden. We could even say it was *instantaneous*. One moment he was well; the next he was ill. Everything was right at ten minutes to one; at nine minutes to one everything was wrong.

The whole world changed within that one moment. Why? Because, through hours, weeks, months, or years he had prepared for it! A steady attrition had continued. He had maintained foolish living habits. He had neglected the common-sense advice about food, exercise, and sleep. But above all, he had worried, fretted, and been irritated; he had allowed himself the luxury of anger; he had accepted a belief in overload; he had disdained spiritual truths; he had refused to apply himself to wisdom. He had drifted into destructive mental habits, gone on emotional binges, refused to fortify himself with positive concepts about his world and his place in it.

Yes, he had prepared himself for it, and when he was sufficiently prepared, it happened. It was instantaneous, but there was a long history of preparation behind it. It occurred in a split second, but something had happened to make it possible.

Could this man, even now, raise himself to the intense clarity of faith where there would be nothing in his consciousness to keep him ill, he could now experience *instantaneous healing*, just as he had experienced *instantaneous illness*.

But such is not likely to be the case, for he has had no such training for healing as he has had for illness. His recovery, if he does recover, must be a thing of medical science, where the *body* is forced to slow down, and allowed to heal, but where the *mind* remains the seed-bed for further illness.

### Don't Wait—Start Now

Because we so seldom can lift ourselves to the intense pitch a perfect faith by which we achieve INSTANTANEOUS HEALING, we must prepare the groundwork in consciousness where such a spasmodic, so-called miraculous, tour-de-force of the spirit will not be necessary. We must prepare ourselves to rise above the human weaknesses that allow an illness to come upon us. It must be a preparation that will enable us to draw upon our acquired knowledge, our understanding and faith, and instantly reverse the manifestations of those human weaknesses.

As we *unconsciously* prepare for our illnesses, we must *consciously* prepare for our healings. So many wait to take a class, to go to church, to read a book. In the summer the leaky roof doesn't need fixing; in the winter it's too late.

There are those who desperately cry out for a miracle, who wonder why an instantaneous healing cannot happen to them. It is because they cannot reach the peak of faith it demands. It is because, in times of health, they did not fortify their own consciousness against the illnesses of this world. It's the old story of the grasshopper and the ant. Elisha revealed the secret when the King asked him to pray for rain to quench the thirst of his troops. "What good is rain," asked Elisha, "if you have nothing in which to hold it? Dig trenches to hold the rain you want."

Prepare! Do not, by default, prepare for disaster, but, by design, prepare for happiness, health, and abundance. Prepare, as well, for the knowledge, understanding, strength, and faith to meet any emergencies. "Prepare ye the way of the Lord." This is an admonition common to the Old Testament and the New. Prepare ye the way for the laws of life to have their harmonious way through you.

## How to Put These Healing Ideas into Action

Continue your essential preparation for INSTANTANEOUS HEAL-
ING by making your next three Idea Cards, and letting their
messages become a dominant part of your consciousness for
at least the next twenty-four hours.

---

### EVENING

*There is a deep, constant, ever-ready power that helps me
meet and overcome every challenge and crisis of life.*
*Tonight my mind prepares itself for the healing I want.*
*Tonight my mind rejects every negative thought and influ-
ence, so that tomorrow my whole life is ready for healing.*
*I believe in my healing. I believe in it for* me.

---

### MORNING

*I give thanks for this new day in which I shall learn some
new thing that prepares me for my healing.*
*I give thanks that somewhere through the night I released
whatever hold I still had on illness.*
*Whether my complete healing occurs today is not important,
because I know that—at the right time—it is inevitable.*
*I know my healing exists. I now prepare for it to demonstrate
itself in me.*

---

### DAY

*I know that I am preparing myself for my healing by reading
and applying this book.*
*I prepare myself by thinking of healing, not of illness;*
*of success, not of failure;*
*of strength, not of weakness.*

*Every moment of this day I am ready to learn new truths,*
*new ideas that will make my preparation for healing*
*complete.*
*I believe in healing.*
*I believe in it for me.*
*I believe in it now.*

•—•—•—•—•—•—•—•—•—•—•—•—•—•—•—•—•—•—•—•—•—•—•—•—•—•—•

# 6

## Use the Law of Primary
## Experience to Achieve Wonders

"It can't be done" is not a statement of truth. It is an acceptance of limitation, and an admission of resignation. The fact
that something has never been done is no indication that it
can't be done. The fact that something has always happened
is no guarantee that it always will or must happen. Principle
is not bound by precedent.

There are certain physical laws that we accept because they
have been taught to us from childhood, and because their
demonstration and proof are obvious. A common example is
the law of gravity. Unless some compensating force or condition is applied to them, things fall earthward. We drop things.
We put things down. We walk; we stand; we lie down. All
this happens, or is made possible, because—whether we like it
or not—all of us are subject to this law of gravity.

### The Laws of Mind Are Unavoidable

There are mental and spiritual laws, too, which also are just
as universal and immutable as any of our physical laws. However, because few of us have ever been taught what they are,

75

and because their demonstration and proof are not so obvious, we fail to recognize that they too, whether we like it or not, are unavoidable in our lives, that we are subject to the laws of mind, just as we are to the laws of physics.

Again let me point out that a man's religion, or lack of it, has no influence or bearing upon any mental or spiritual laws. The laws of mind work anywhere, at any time, and for any person. The laws of water are not concerned with who drinks the water, or who drowns in it. They are neutral, and that's all there is to it. It is the same with the laws of mind. We cannot, because we profess a certain philosophy or religion, claim them as exclusively our own, nor can we for the same reason escape them.

You may say that the principles given in this book are religious, or spiritual. You are right. Yet, they embrace all religions without being limited to any particular one. Mental and spiritual laws cannot be segregated. In them there is no discrimination. From them there is no immunity. Just as there is no doctrine in physical laws, so there is none in the laws of mind.

If you or I wanted a drink of water we would get a glass, go to the sink, turn on the faucet, fill the glass, and drink the water. But let's imagine a man who walks into the house and knows nothing about modern plumbing. He has never seen a faucet, and does not associate it with water. If he is thirsty, even desperately thirsty, he will be within a few feet of that which can quench his thirst, yet he will not know it, and he will remain thirsty.

This is but a simple parallel to the condition, we might even say ignorance, of much of the world today. The power it needs to free itself of fear, conflict, pain and suffering is within the instant reach of its own thought, yet it seems unable to achieve it. Its spiritual, mental, and moral thirst goes unquenched, and as a consequence, life dries up, falls sick, withers into mediocrity and dull routine. The difficulty with this world is that it has failed to learn how to turn on that power. It knows too much about what *can't* happen, and too little about what *can*.

### The Law of Primary (First) Experience

There is a law of mind which has been called "The Law of Primary Experience." It can be stated a different way by saying, "Principle is not bound by precedent," or another way by saying, "There is always a first (primary) time for everything." The fact that something always has been done is no guarantee that it must or will be done. Your attention has been called and will be called to this law in relation to various circumstances relating to healing.

This law applies not only to the world, but to each person individually. "It can't be done," says one man. Don't you believe him! "It's never been done," says another. "So what?" you can reply.

Consider the remarkable achievements of science in connection with the human body itself:

A woman in Detroit lives today because every time her heart-beat opens a valve, a small watch-spring sewed into her heart closes it.

A man in Santa Monica returned to work having survived 36 complete stoppages of his heart in 24 hours. An electrical mechanism supplied heartbeats until his own resumed.

Although a million-to-one seem almost impossible odds, a baby beat those odds not long ago. Lorna Hazelwood was born in Southern California on January 7, 1961. She arrived three months and ten days early. After ten days she weighed one and one-half pounds. Furthermore, the mother's case-history was against the baby girl, since three brothers and sisters had been either stillborn or premature, the latter dying in infancy. "No chance," said the doctors, "or at best one in a million." However, when they finally concluded that the child was going to live, they advised the parents that it would take their daughter five or six years to catch up with children born at the full term. Yet, at two years the child weighed twenty-eight pounds, and was either caught up with or ahead of (both physically and mentally) other children her own age.

A nine-year-old Arkansas girl becomes a mother, while an Englishwoman of seventy-five dies in pregnancy.

But these, you say (and rightly), can be attributed to natural responses and scientific help. Nevertheless, we must agree that they are *beyond and above* the "normal expectancy," or the "average experience." Ordinarily, they wouldn't happen, or they couldn't happen, *but they did.*

What about the British airman, whose heart stopped for eighty-six minutes? He was revived, and he lived. Or the eighty-four year old man in San Jose, California who grew his third set of teeth?

A 39-year old man in Cleveland lost half his brain in an operation, yet retained much of his comprehension and intelligence as if no operation had been performed.

A news story tells of a sixty-year-old woman, blind since she was nine weeks old, who suddenly regained her sight. What about her?

Would you have said that these things could not happen?

If you are facing something that seems impossible, or a million-to-one, something that has never been done before, or always eluded you, something in which others predict you will fail, or even that you have tried and failed before, remember this Law of Primary Experience: "Principle is not bound by precedent."

### No "Giving Up"

Some friends of a young man of 21 wrote to our Service of Healing, asking treatment for him through that department and our Sunday services. The young man is employed by the Parks and Recreation Department of a western city. He was an athletic instructor, and was coaching basketball when he collapsed, and was taken to the hospital. He hadn't felt well for some time, but had ignored the warnings. The diagnosis was leukemia.

He was transferred to a hospital specializing in his disease, and placed in the isolation ward. The verdict: two weeks to live.

Following his first few physical treatments, his entire body became swollen. Great sores appeared upon it. The news reached his friends in the recreation department. "He was a nice fellow," they said. They spoke of him in the past tense.

The woman charged with programming certain activities in the park and recreation department which included this young man was advised of the verdict. In spite of this, under instructions from the Service of Healing, and following her own knowledge of treatment procedures, she too refused to accept it. When negative beliefs arose, she denied and rejected them as having any reality. She declared, as did we, that he would soon be well again, as indeed he already was well in mind. She kept in contact with his mother to give her encouragement, and requested permission to write the boy each day and ask when he would be ready to return to his duties. She wrote the doctor to get permission to assign him to a summer schedule. She notified the boy of this arrangement, and told him she expected him to meet it. All this time, according to those in charge of his physical body, he was dying. Then, only a few days later, another routine test was taken. His blood count was normal. He was healed.

One week later he was discharged. Today he is back on the job, an example of strength and health. He has reported regularly to the hospital. No trace of the disease remains, a disease that was supposed to kill him in short order.

"I was sure scared," he admitted later. "I didn't know what to do. Then, on a Sunday morning, I suddenly felt a calmness, and somehow I just knew I was going to get well. I can't explain it, but I just knew it. And I wasn't worried any more."

### If You Want Precedents, You Have Them

The healing of a certain dread illness may seem impossible, yet if you want them, there are positive precedents to show it is not. A peculiar characteristic of human nature makes us have more confidence in something if we know it already has been accomplished. For thousands of years man was not able to run a mile in under four minutes. But when Roger Bannister broke that four-minute mile, everyone suddenly knew it could be done. And it has been done numerous times since then. Fifteen feet was once considered the absolute limit for the pole vault. That height is now the province of the second-rate competitors.

You might begin your own treatment for the "impossible" by saying, "If anyone can be healed of this, I can be healed of it." Whatever condition it is you want—happiness, healing, love, or success—there are numberless precedents to prove that it can be achieved. Each one of us was created by the same intelligence. There were no limitations placed upon us or special dispensations given to any of us at birth. The Infinite is as interested in you as in anyone else who was ever born. If it can happen anywhere, it can happen to you.

"I feel good for two or three days and then I am miserable again," someone will complain. If it is possible to feel good one day or one hour, then it is possible to feel good for any extended time. One hour has demonstrated the capacity, the potential.

### Freedom from the Past—Freedom for the Future

Now we move one step further toward the effective application of the Law of Primary Experience. "Principle is not bound by precedent," it tells us. Again this works two ways:

1. The fact that something never happened in the past is no proof that it cannot happen now. This truth frees us for the *future* in which to achieve what we can conceive.

2. The fact that something did happen in the past is no proof that it must happen again. This truth frees us from the *past*, from the fear of any "unbreakable" record, from averages, normals, and statistics.

The real message of this law is this: Look to today; plan for tomorrow; do not be bound by what happened or failed to happen yesterday. When we accept this, and follow it, we are freed of the past, both in our personal experiences and in the records and experiences of the world. There is always a first time for everything!

At one time all the great record-holders took the first, uncertain, faltering steps of a child. Someone first used fire as a friend. Someone first saw the possibilities of the wheel. Someone first conceived the idea of flight. These were all breakthroughs into areas that had been "impossible." Perhaps their first concepts were thought too good to be true. But *nothing* is too good to be true. What man can conceive, he can achieve. At one time these things couldn't happen, *but they did!*

What would you think if I were to tell you that a simple, basically uneducated girl, working as a dressmaker in the garment district of one of our big cities is going to get a personal interview with the President of the United States, convince him that he should give her command of the military forces of the United States, and get him to send her on a campaign against world Communism, which she will win? "Impossible!" you will say. "It couldn't happen." Yet, here is what John Steinbeck, in the *Saturday Review*, says of Joan of Arc: [1]

"The story of Joan could not possibly have happened—and did. . . . Joan is a fairytale so improbable that, without the most

---

[1] John Steinbeck, "The Joan in All of Us," *Saturday Review*, Jan. 14, 1956, p. 17. Copyright 1956 by John Steinbeck.

complete historical record and evidence, it could not be believed." Yet it happened.

Whatever the "voices" Joan heard may have been, they convinced her that she was right, that she could not fail, that she was to be the saviour of France. She was prepared in consciousness. She expected victory. She believed in it for her.

*It couldn't happen, but it did!*

### Learn That Nothing Is Impossible

The Law of Primary Experience speaks of *primary* (the *first*) experience. You need no precedent. Why? Because "with God all things are possible." "If God be for us, who can be against us?"

And where is God? Up there? Out here? Near? Far? The answer is, "The Kingdom of God is within." You have the power within. The power is within you, whether you use it for yourself or direct it to others.

At a dinner party recently a woman told me she was the daughter of a minister. When she was a little girl, her father received a message that a woman in his parish was dying. The girl knew this woman, she knew how happy she and her husband had been. Why should this woman die when she was so happy?

As her father was preparing to go to the woman's house to give his final blessings to her, and comfort to her bereaved husband, the girl asked her father, "Why not pray for Mrs. Green?" For some reason unknown to the girl, her father said something about "the will of God," and spoke as if the woman's death had already taken place. When he left, however, the girl went upstairs and prayed. It was the first time she had ever prayed for someone else. "I just knew Mrs. Green was well!" she exclaimed.

When her father returned, he looked at her and said, "Something very strange has happened. Mrs. Green is well." The woman at the dinner party said that she never told her father of what she had done, because she didn't want to interfere with his concept of the will of God.

One evening I received a call from a man who had just been summoned by the doctor and told that his sister had no more than three hours to live. I treated for her immediately. I denied the verdict that had been reached for her, and claimed healing and health. Four hours later, as soon as I could leave my class, I went to the famous medical clinic where she had been taken. The halls were dark, but when I went into her room she was awake. We talked quietly for a few minutes. She was alert, and responsive. I told her that I was knowing for her all the basic truths so necessary to her healing. I explained them briefly. Her attitude was excellent. There was no doubt in her own mind about her recovery. When I left I said, "I'll see you in a few days."

Later that week her brother called and said the doctors could not explain what had happened that night, that suddenly she was better, and was well enough to go home.

She told her brother that during the night ropes had seemed to be reaching out to her, and at the end of each rope were the faces of her family and of me. Later she told me, "I remembered one thing you had said to me: 'Act as if it were impossible to fail!'"

The medical staff asked her to stay a few extra days so that they could make tests to find out what happened. They were so puzzled, and so overwhelmed by even her survival through the night, that word of it spread throughout the hospital, and newspapers and radio the following afternoon reported it. Missing was an account of her midnight talk with me. That, however, is unimportant. What is important is that according to the best medical opinion, *it couldn't happen, but it did!*

*You* are as much a part of the Divine principles of healing as anyone else. The Law of Primary Experience applies to *you*. Nothing is bound by the past. Precedent or not, even if it has never happened, *know that it can happen for you!* This is the third secret of INSTANTANEOUS HEALING.

### Putting These Healing Ideas into Action

You are now about to make your seventh set of Idea Cards. Are you really *using* them? Are you *living* their ideas, or are you merely reading and repeating them? Day by day, if you have followed them closely, you have been coming nearer that INSTANTANEOUS HEALING.

No matter what you do for the next twenty-four hours, live, act, work, talk, think, buy, sell, travel, play, or rest in the constant awareness of what you have been directed to claim for yourself by your Idea Cards. Do nothing and *think* nothing which is in conflict with them.

Check everything you do or think against the messages of your cards. If it is in conflict with them, *reject* it; *refuse* to do it or think it. *Nothing* and *no one* can *make* you accept any negative or destructive idea as true for *you*.

●-●-●-●-●-●-●-●-●-●-●-●-●-●-●-●-●-●-●-●-●-●-●-●-●-●-●-●-●-●-●-●-●-●-●-●-●-●-●

## EVENING

*My mind knows that I can be healed.*

*There is no truth in the words "It can't be done."*

*Sometime, somewhere in this world, every illness has been healed.*

> *If it can happen anywhere, it can happen for me, because I am no different from anyone else.*

> *Every law of this world acts for me, just as it acts for anyone else.*

*Tonight I leave my past. In my sleep I leave the old patterns of illness. Tomorrow I awaken a new person.*

●-●-●-●-●-●-●-●-●-●-●-●-●-●-●-●-●-●-●-●-●-●-●-●-●-●-●-●-●-●-●-●-●-●-●-●-●-●-●

MORNING

> *Today I am a new person.*
> *All the old illness patterns are gone. They just fell away from me in the night.*
> *I know that my health is true.*
> *I go to meet my new, healthy self in everything I do and am today.*

<hr />

DAY

> *Health is happening for me.*
> *Every cell in my body is being renewed and strengthened every moment of this day.*
> *I am now enjoying the health that my new faith tells me is mine.*
> *All day long my body responds to my discovery of this truth "It can happen to me!"*
> *It is happening now.*

<hr />

# 7

## How to Face Healing Reality, While Turning Your Back on Destructive Fact

FACT: We are Our *Bodies*.
TRUTH: We are Our *Minds*.

Who are we? We are our minds. We do not see with our eyes, smell with our nose, hear with our ears, taste with our tongue, touch with our fingers, or think with our brain. We do all these things with mind, through these material things. They are only the tools. Hammers and saws do not build a house; the mind directing them builds it.

If our minds are anesthetized or eliminated in some way, we do not experience. Mind is that *by* which we experience; body is that *through* which we experience.

A woman who could "hear voices" came to see me. She didn't mind "hearing" them, but she wanted to understand them. I asked her if she had a favorite flower. "Yes," she said, "gardenias." I told her to close her eyes and imagine that she was smelling a gardenia. We waited a few seconds. "Can you smell it now?" I asked. "Oh, yes," she answered, "very well!"

Each of the senses acts just as strangely under certain conditions. Some fire- or asphyxiation-conscious persons can "smell gas" or "smoke" almost anywhere. If you ever have been hungry for a long space of time, do you remember thinking about a good steak and being able to "smell" it? At times you may even have been able to "taste" it. Think of pulling a knife or string between your teeth. Think of scratching your fingernail on a blackboard. Does this send shivers down your spine, or give you "goose-bumps?" You know that nothing physical happened. There was no knife, no string, no blackboard. Yet, a physical reaction took place. The mind alone created the physical sensation.

However, the mind is also the origin (the creator) of other conditions which do exist, which do have reality, conditions which begin as a thought (emotion), and end as a physical thing. It is important for each of us to know the difference; in other words, what is fact and what is "reality"; which reactions are based upon the truth, and which are based upon that which only seems to be the truth?

### The Reality of Mental-Spiritual Healing

It is surprising how often the newspapers refer to the truth about the powers of the mind as something "new," as if for centuries the world had been living under the facts of illness, while the truths of healing are only now being discovered. To read the headlines one might be led to believe that the use of the mind in healing is a recent development. For instance, here are three examples of hundreds of such headlines:

NEW CURE FOR ARTHRITIS MAY BE FOUND IN
EASING TENSIONS

NEW AIDS TO LONG LIFE DISCOVERED
IN A QUIET MIND

ALLERGY SUFFERERS GET NEW HELP
FROM MENTAL CLINIC

In spite of emphasis on the word "new," the healing power of the Mind has been known and used for centuries. Mind is the great physician. This truth is not new. The following quotations demonstrate its timelessness and universality:

400 B.C.:

> We do not cure the body with the body; we cure the body with the *Mind;* and if the mind is confused and upset, it cannot cure anything properly.
>
> Plato, The Republic

300 B.C.:

> ...as he thinketh in his heart, so is he.
>
> Proverbs

30 A.D.:

> If anyone consults a doctor after the age of 30, he is a fool, since by that time everyone should know how to regulate his life properly.
>
> Tiberius

30 A.D.:

> According to your faith be it unto you.
> All things are possible to him that believeth.
> A good tree cannot bring forth evil fruit, neither can a corrupt tree bring forth good fruit.
> Wherefore by their fruits ye shall know them.
>
> Jesus

175 A.D.:

> If you are pained by any external thing, it is not this that disturbs you, but your own judgment about it.
>
> Marcus Aurelius

1096 A.D.:

> Robert, Duke of Normandy, had ample reason to reflect upon the causes in a man's life, and how to avoid the dangerous ones when, after recovering from both love and

a sword wound in Italy where he had gone with the Crusaders, he spent 28 years in an English prison upon his return home. His brother feared that Robert had intentions to seize the throne. While in prison Robert wrote his famous *Regimen Sanitatus* in Latin. In it he included some of the first hints of what was to flower into psychosomatic medicine. It was not until 500 years after his death, however, that his work was accepted. This was in

1607 A.D.:

The year in which *Regimen Sanitatus,* translated by Sir John Harrington, went into 240 editions. Here are two examples of what it contained:

Use three physicians still,
First, Doctor Quiet;
Next, Doctor Merry-man;
And then, Doctor Diet.

Joy, Temperance and Repose
Slam the door on the doctor's nose.

1540 A.D.:

Heavy thoughts bring on physical maladies. When the soul is oppressed, so is the body.

Martin Luther

1552 A.D.:

Our bodies cannot . . . be hurt by corrupt and ineffective causes, except there be in them a certain matter apt to receive it, else if *one* were sick, *all* should be sick.

John Caius

1950's A.D.:

Dr. Ian Stevenson, psychiatrist as well as teacher of medicine, writing in *Harper's Magazine* says,

Recent work has demonstrated the great significance of emotional factors in heart-failure and diabetes. Indeed there now remains no organ of the body in which physical changes related to emotions have not been proved of major importance.[1]

Today all diseases are psychosomatic. We have to treat the man, not pieces and parts.[2]

1960's A.D.:

The following are among other headlines taken from America's newspapers during the past 10 years:

TENSION: KILLER OF MIND, BODY

ILLNESS, DEATH LINKED
TO RUNAWAY EMOTIONS

ARTHRITIS LINKED TO EMOTIONAL STRESS

MENTAL STRESS BLAMED
FOR ULCERATIVE COLITIS

EMOTIONS AS WELL AS DIET CAUSE
TOOTH DECAY, RESEARCH INDICATES

EMOTIONAL PATTERN TOLD HEART ATTACK
"CANDIDATES"

OVER HALF DISEASES DUE TO EMOTIONS

EMOTIONS BLAMED FOR 70% of PATIENTS' ILLS

PSYCHOSOMATIC FACTOR SEEN IN ALL
DISEASE BY MEDICAL RESEARCH TEAM

Despite the long, even ancient history of man's realization of the psychosomatic factors in his illnesses, public education and acceptance is just now beginning to acknowledge the

---

[1] Ian Stevenson, "Psychosomatic Medicine, Part I," *Harper's Magazine,* July 1954, p. 37.

[2] Dr. William C. Menninger, Menninger Clinic, Topeka, Kansas. (*Newsweek,* Dec. 8, 1958.)

reality that *illnesses begin in the mind.* One day it will also acknowledge the reality that healing, as well, begins in the mind.

### It's Your Choice

If every man whose wife passed on, whose business went bankrupt, whose body was attacked by a certain disease— if every person faced with a big decision, caught in a crisis, left with some staggering load reacted in *exactly the same way,* in other words—came to the same conclusions, reached the same decisions, achieved the same results, then something terrible would have happened to man to make him remain subject to his problems, without the choice of thought or action to meet and overcome them.

Even so, men sometimes seek the "standard" way, the "proven," "safe" way, and neglect or refuse to employ a bold, yet creative way to meet their challenges and solve their problems. Nothing has power over any of us unless consciously, or sub-consciously, we give it that power. Every hardship, trouble, challenge, or tragedy is relative. Of itself it possesses nothing with which it is not endowed by the consciousness (the mind) which observes and reacts to it. Its power is relative only to that consciousness (mind) which recognizes and accepts it. Otherwise, it does not exist, or it exists only as an occurrence, without power or significance.

I have often had to point out to a client that he is giving more weight and power to his problems than they deserve. This is not an easy declaration to make about someone else's troubles, because it gives him the opportunity of charging you with underestimating his problem simply because it is not your own. To say that another's problem has been blown up beyond its importance or value is to court that other's anger, irritation, or impatience. The response to such a declaration usually is, "But Doctor Smith—you've got to face reality!"

When someone says, "But I've got to be realistic!" or, "I've got to face reality!", usually he means only "I've got to face the *facts!*" This is because he has not discovered that facts are different for everyone, while *for everyone reality is exactly the same.*

It is *reality* by which, through which, and under which we reach an awareness of an Infinite power within ourselves, which may be directed into all our experiences. On the other hand it is the *facts* of our individual lives by which, through which, and under which we surrender ourselves to the errors, untruths, and penalties of our problems.

*We are being truly realistic only when we do not give our problems the power that, of themselves, they do not possess.*

### Reality Cannot Be Distorted

Each one of us lives in the midst of a different combination of facts. Among them may be a serious eye condition, heart trouble, a pending operation for malignancy, or an infection of some kind. There is only one thing with which to face these facts: *reality!*

Some would like to reverse the process, and confront reality with the fact of their illness, their loneliness, age, financial status, or unhappiness. But it can't be done. The only thing they succeed in doing is to force themselves to observe, agree with, and give power to their factual problem.

We cannot distort reality. We can distort only our image of reality, so that life seems hard, God seems cruel, and suffering seems inevitable. But life is not hard, God is not cruel, and suffering is not inevitable. They only appear to be so when we are too willing to accept them as so.

Our knowledge of both facts and reality is almost inexhaustible. Facts change, however, while reality is constant. Reality is that which was, is, and will be. It cannot be changed. Only one's view of it can be warped. Only one's understanding of it can be faulty.

Therefore, in the challenges and crises of life, we must fortify ourselves with reality, not with facts.

### Put the Emphasis in the Right Place

It has been said before that somewhere in this world every known illness has been healed. Often we call these healings "miracles," meaning something supernatural or abnormal. But the "miracle," so-called, is reality, while the illness was only error, a temporal fact.

When we doubt the reality of the Infinite in which there is no illness, we doubt our claim to that illness-free reality. To put it differently, we repeat that there is no illness, no disease in God. How do we know this? It is from the wisdom of the ages. But when we put emphasis on the weaknesses of the self rather than on the strengths of the Infinite (God) within, we distort this wisdom, and thus live by the fact of our weaknesses, rather than by the reality of our strengths.

Let us say that George Jameson is ill. He faces this fact fortified with reality, the knowledge that this illness has been healed. He knows, then, that whatever this illness may be, it is not impregnable, undefeatable, incurable. Others may tell him that his illness dooms him. But George knows that the evidence will not support the claim to its unavoidably fatal reputation. With this knowledge, George possesses one of the secrets of INSTANTANEOUS HEALING.

### Don't Overlook Even These Small Realities

Statistics make facts and facts only. Ninety-nine per cent over 500,000 years is not good enough evidence to support the contention that the remaining 1% is "miraculous," that according to "the laws of nature" it never should have happened. If the man who faces his illness takes this 1% as a demonstration of the reality it is, he is already on his way to healing. If he takes it as an improbable or impossible figure insofar as *he* is concerned, he is turning his back on a human potential, and an Infinite reality. *Face the fact of illness with the reality of healing and of health. Do not look upon these things as longed-for but unreachable conditions in your life.*

## How to Reach Your Transition Points

So many say, "We've got to face reality," when they mean only that they have to face the facts of this moment. The facts of this moment, however, are only the "transition points" where the past (whatever it was) becomes the future (whatever it may be).

How much weight, value, importance, and influence are you at this moment giving to the facts of your life? Among them may be the loss of a loved one, the lack of education, a physical handicap, an epidemic, a disappointment, your age. How devastating, humiliating, limiting or intimidating are you allowing these to be to you? These are the facts so many are referring to when they protest, "But I've got to face reality!" These are the occurrences and conditions which so many are prone to invest with power they do not contain of themselves. Consequently, these occurrences and conditions become the ruling facts of their lives, instead of the transition points at which they break through to the reality of happiness, health, fulfillment, and peace.

Now why do we insist that we make more of our problems than they deserve? Because, as Tiberius pointed out almost 2,000 years ago, all problems are reflections of the spiritually immature; in the light of reality, they have no weight, authority, influence, or value at all.

The man who is truly aware of the power of the Infinite in him, gives less importance to his problems than does the man who is not aware of that power. He does not ignore them, but at the same time, he does not succumb to them. He faces them, but he faces them with reality.

### You Are Reality

To the person who says, "But Dr. Smith, I've got to face reality!" I can only say, "*You* are reality, you are eternal, giving power to a temporal fact. It is reality you must use in order to face and to overcome the facts, the transition points between what was, what is, and what you want to be."

All men and women are exposed to disease, but only some prove susceptible. Only some contract disease, and only part of these succumb. Why? Because through his thinking, man makes himself either immune or susceptible to disease and to its results. This has become almost the major axiom of psychosomatic medicine.

The word psychosomatic is made up of two words—"psyche," meaning *mind*, and "soma," meaning *body*. There is a definite, irrevocable relationship between the two. Thought is the key to man's health. Thought is energy. It is the wrong use of energy that causes man to break down. The second Law of Thermodynamics (simplified) says that everything tends to run down. Nothing that we yet know of is perfectly (100%) efficient. This includes both the mind and the body.

In the engine it is friction, the energy dissipated in noncreative channels, that causes it to break down. In man it is also friction, although we may call it by different names, that causes him to break down. Destructive attitudes and emotions (sustained or chronic) such as fear, worry, hatred, jealousy, envy, anxiety, hostility, irritation, and resentment are only a few of the frictions in thinking which cause breakdowns in the body.

When energy is used through such destructive mental activity, the body does not function efficiently, and begins to break down. As any or all of those negative attitudes, emotions, and beliefs are used in greater intensity, with more regularity, and in more dangerous combinations, the more serious and seemingly "incurable" can the illness or disease become.

On the other hand, when the thinking is lifted, cleansed of its negativity, is harmonious and at peace—even though that "peace" is a challenging, busy, dynamic peace—it is operating more efficiently, and consequently not only prevents illness, but establishes the atmosphere in which illness can be healed.

We can read this truth between the lines in a news story. What made the story "news" was the realization that a human verdict was countermanded by some higher, Divine decision. The headline read: "LEUKEMIA VICTIM CURED MYSTE-RIOUSLY."

The original report had been printed in the Journal of the American Medical Association. A 54-year-old woman in the Lenox Hill Hospital, New York, showed the clear and unmistakable signs of her dreaded disease: the hardened, swollen spleen, the swollen lymph glands, the blood-riddled cells; her weight was down forty pounds; she was pale and weak. Dr. Carl Reich, her blood specialist for two years, had injected potions, sprayed with X-rays, and changed her blood, all without results. He gave her the verdict. "You now have six months to live."

The woman thought this over, and made a decision. "I want to see Ireland again before I die."

Since she was able to move about, but was going to die anyway, the doctor saw no reason why she should not go.

She returned the following August. Immediately she went to Dr. Reich for an examination. All signs of leukemia had disappeared. In September the doctor saw her again, although he had never expected to do so. He took every test of tissue, blood, and marrow, yet not one indication of the disease remained. The doctor and the hospital staff could only speculate through their amazement.

What we do not know, of course, was what emotional change took place in this woman. Did the trip to Ireland free her of old fears, of loneliness, of a feeling of separation, of a belief of being in the wrong place, of a belief in wrong action? There seems little question but that this was so. In some way we may never know, her *thoughts* were healed. She thus became a perfect channel for the healing of the *body*. It was not geography that healed her, but a release from some old, sickening thought. When this happened, the human verdict (death in six months) was overruled by a Divine decision (health and life).

This woman's experience proved once again that there are no incurable diseases. But of course some will say that her healing was only an isolated, unique case. Was it? We must admit it is unusual, so unusual that it received world-wide publicity. But it is not unique. It is not isolated, nor even mysterious.

## Avoid the Recurrence of Destructive Thought

Eight years ago a man who came to see me also had leukemia. A corps of doctors pronounced the human verdict. We worked; we treated; we prayed. What was the final decision? He was healed. All tests showed there were no remaining signs.

However, while the consciousness was lifted enough for the healing, life's problems grew heavy for this man. Two years later he suffered a stroke, a physical breakdown. Again, what was the human verdict? He wouldn't recover. We worked; we treated; we prayed. What was the final decision? He made a quick recovery and went back to work.

Once again, pressure of responsibility became grave. The following year he suffered a coronary thrombosis. What was the human verdict? He wouldn't recover. Again we worked. What was the final decision? Recovery. He went back to work. He was shaken, but he did recover.

Why were we able to over-rule those three human verdicts? Because we relied on a Divine decision, and each time *we cleared his thoughts.*

Why did he slip back into illness? There was a recurrence of pressure, renewed tension, a new practice of destructive thinking.

If he does not finally and successfully overcome his tendency to slip back into the "friction-thoughts," one day a human verdict will come true, and those who could not believe in his healings will say, "I told you so!"

## Stand in the Presence of the Healing Power

Stories of healing usually reveal that those who were healed began, at some point, to face reality, not the facts. The facts were threatening. In the facts they found fear, foreboding, defeat. The facts told them about the "incurable," set time-limits on life, warned them of impending disaster. But when they turned away from the facts and faced *reality*, they saw life in a new perspective. They felt hope; they found a new faith; they *believed* in their healing. For when they faced reality, they were in the presence of the only true Healing Power there is. They placed themselves *above* the human verdicts, and accepted only a Divine decision that recognized no limiting, final, inevitable facts.

With your discovery, understanding, and acceptance of each succeeding Secret, you are drawing closer to your own INSTANTANEOUS HEALING. No matter what facts you have been told, be sure that you face reality, that you know the truth about the Healing Power in you. Then the "hopeless" conditions of life are hopeless no longer. Then you are started on the road to recovery and well being.

Make your cards—or mark this place, and put these healing ideas into *action:*

<hr />

## EVENING

*I know that I have been giving my problems power over me
by making them more important than they are.*

*Tonight I stop struggling with them. I release them to that
Infinite Solver of all questions, and I sleep in peace.*

<hr />

## MORNING

*This morning—with all its freshness, newness, and promise—
is my reality.*

*The fears, the worries of yesterday were only dreams.*

*They drifted away in the night. They were false, untrue.*

*From this moment on, I will not let my mind be taken over
by any destructive thought.*

<hr />

## DAY

*Today I recognize the one Infinite Reality in which there is
no disease.*

*I am part of that Reality. Therefore, I refuse to accept any
illness as true for me—it is only the image of a false idea.*

*Today I express the strengths of life—hope, love, courage,
thankfulness, thoughtfulness, helpfulness. I build on these;
I make these the basis of everything I do and am today.*

<hr />

# 8

## How to Use the Law of the Normal Standard to Achieve "Miracles" and Get What You Want Out of Life

An amusing little "miracle" happened in Pasadena, California a year or two ago. A woman who had raised 148 dogs finally found one which didn't follow the normal pattern. An eight-year-old Springer spaniel named Gay was the mother of two-year-old Sukey. Sukey had a litter of pups, but appeared somewhat surprised when her own mother moved in and began helping her nurse them. The pups fared equally well on the nourishment from mother or grandmother. Authorities on dogs said it was impossible at her age, but Gay—by human standards 56 years old—didn't know it was impossible. She had no way of knowing that lactation just couldn't happen in a dog which at the time had not gone through an actual gestation period. During her daughter's gestation and delivery, however, her maternal instincts and desires were so great that she believed herself capable of nursing them, *and she was*. In her own dog's consciousness, it was perfectly normal for her to do so. She wasn't in the least concerned by the veterinarian's pronouncement that it wasn't normal for her to become, if not in fact, at least in appearances and feeding powers, a mother again. Although she was supposed to act as all "normal" dogs would act, she was not aware of this. She refused to be limited by what she was "not supposed" to be able to do. She went about setting her own "normal," and *life responded in her* to satisfy it.

This surge of life, this power to help us rise above the normals that the world's "authorities" set for us, waits only for us to establish the normals that we *want* and *can believe in for ourselves.*

Out of this truth we have discovered what is called the Law of the Normal Standard. *What we believe is normal for us tends to become normal for us.*

## Why the Errors Have Become the Normal

It has often been said that it is easier to accept and to believe a lie that one has heard a thousand times, than to accept and to believe a truth that one has just heard for the first time. This is why the lies and errors of life usually have become the normal, while truth has remained the rare, the unique, the abnormal. This is why we have a body of professional errors which lists certain diseases as incurable. This is why there are those who say, "My age is against me"; "war is inevitable"; "you can't change human nature"; "all the great opportunities are gone." Men begin to accept these things as normal for them, and inevitably they become normal for them.

"Normals" often are created on the basis of peculiar and unusual circumstances. It may take only one isolated experience to so impress something upon one's mind that it is accepted as normal, and thereafter tends to become normal.

## What Kind of Normals Have You Set?

You may have established an unwanted normal in your life on the basis of some solitary or unique experience. Whether this is good or bad depends, of course, upon the kind and quality of that normal, whether it restricts and harms you, or frees and helps you. The value or danger of any normal, sub-normal, or abnormal depends upon what that normal is. Many of the accepted normals of the world are vicious and destructive, or at least useless and non-productive.

Also, there are normals that begin as happy and constructive ones, but which turn into unhappy, negative ones. For example, the growing boy whose normal breakfast and eating capacity is three eggs, ten hotcakes, and five slices of bacon might do well to establish a lower normal when his growing is ended; whereas, the boy whose normal earning capacity is five dollars a week would do well to establish a higher normal when he becomes a man.

Whenever you allow yourself to become attached to a normal you do not want, you are slowing down the creative processes of your own mind. It is then that you should know and understand the Law of the Normal Standard: *That which you accept and believe as normal for you begins to become normal for you.*

### How You Can Spot Those Who Are Setting Poor Normals

The establishment and acceptance of undesirable normals is demonstrated every day by those who say: "I can't make any more money in my business." "I'm past the age where I can expect love, happiness, health, or a job." "There's always been something wrong with me, and there always will be. I'm just the sick type." "I'll never be able to have the things Joe has." Men and women who believe these self-told lies set them as their normals—and life responds.

Hundreds of thousands are going through life living in a permanent state of illness because they have come to believe that illness is just their normal condition of life. The plain truth is that we shall never consistently experience above the level of health we consider normal for us.

### Arnold Palmer's "Normal"

Arnold Palmer loses his share of golf tournaments, but as far as the other professional golfers are concerned, he wins more than his share. When Palmer went to London to play in the British open, he was interviewed by a reporter from the London *Observer*.[1] In his self-analysis, Palmer gave two reasons for his phenomenal and consistent success: 1. *Total concentration*, and 2. *Belief that he will win.*

It was pointed out that "the professional tournament golfers were beginning to get the message that there is something about Palmer's golf that transcends his admitted ability to hit the ball exceedingly well." Whenever he loses his concentration, or begins to doubt that he will win, he loses the tournament, or has to make a spectacular change of attitude, and a comeback to pull victory out of the fire.

What is it in his attitude that transcends mere technical ability? It is his persistent belief that "a shot that had to succeed would succeed." Palmer himself has said that he never makes a tournament shot he doesn't expect to be good.

"A lot of people criticize the way I gamble on a risky shot when I'm in trouble," he said. "I'll be in the woods somewhere, and there will be just this little opening between branches in the direction of the hole. Whereas a safe way out would allow me to avoid further damage, and sacrifice only a stroke, I'm almost always sure to play through the small opening. The reason I do it is that I honestly believe it will work."

Palmer says that he begins mental preparation before he begins play. "I arrange to shut out everything that might get in my way—doubts, worries, other players," he says. "It is arranged for on the conscious level but it produces effects on the sub-

---

[1] Alfred Wright, Jr., "The Incredible Arnold Palmer," *The Continental Magazine*, Vol. 3, No. 1, Feb.-Mar. 1963, pp. 4-5.

conscious level. You just feel right, though you don't know why or what you feel right about."

Arnold Palmer's method includes:

1. Concentration—shutting out all distractions.
2. Mental preparation.
3. Believing in victory as an accepted, normal thing.

The Law of the Normal Standard works for you, just as it does for Arnold Palmer. No man is denied the benefit of the law, and no man is immune.

### Eight Suggestions for Improving Your Own Normals

1. Act and think as if it were impossible for you to fail.
2. Tell yourself that nothing can keep you from your goal.
3. Picture health, not illness.
4. How would you feel if you were well? *Use* your imagination.
5. Refuse to accept any substitutes for healing as "just as good." Accept less than you want—relief or ease of pain—only as a way point that you may be using on your journey to permanent healing.
6. Stop thinking of healing as unusual.
7. Don't blindly accept all the old, stock answers for attempted healings that failed.
8. If, up to now, you've never experienced the health you want, begin thinking of it as normal now, just as the date on which you are reading this book is normal for this day.

### Why Miracles Happen Every Day

If you do not believe in miracles, you are rare. If you do not believe in miracles, and do not want to, you are rarer still. It is fascinating to turn our imagination to some possible miracle

that could make our lives suddenly so much better. So many
pray that a miracle will happen to them to bring riches, allevi-
ate pain, overcome loneliness. So many find pleasure in imagin-
ing that a supernatural force will choose them through which
to work its wonders. "But," they so often sigh, "miracles don't
happen."

Webster's dictionary says that a "miracle is an event or effect
in the physical world deviating from known laws of nature, or
transcending our knowledge of these laws."

Here is a significant point. Man's human knowledge becomes
the standard by which he decides something is miraculous. In
other words, that which happens in accordance with what he
knows of the laws of nature (God) he can accept as commonplace or even as rare, but certainly not as miraculous. However,
anything which happens in accordance with laws of nature
(God) about which he knows nothing, he calls miraculous,
because he judges events through his own limited knowledge
of the magnitude and range of both spiritual and physical laws.

If a wise man of ancient Greece were to see our motion pictures today—their movement, color and sound, their bigger-
than-life figures—he would think of them as miraculous, while
we know enough about the laws of such things to accept them
as wonderful and entertaining, but hardly miraculous.

If the savage thought in such terms, he might look up at a
plane flying over his hut and call what he sees a miracle, while
the pilot, flying in a knowledge of the laws of flight, might think
of it as a wonderful experience, but not a miracle, or as something supernatural.

Jesus said, "He that believeth on me, the works that I do
he shall do also, and greater works than these shall he do."
While everyone else was calling them miracles, he was calling
his healings simply his "work." Jesus knew and practiced the
healing art because he understood the mental-spiritual laws
governing healing. Jesus was the Christ-principle personified.
This Christ-principle is the spiritual center in every person. It is

in you who are reading this book, whatever name you wish to call it. When you are ready to believe in this high spiritual consciousness within yourself ("He that believeth on me . . .") you, too, are ready to do such healing work. This book is written in an awareness and understanding of this power within you, and it explains the secrets through which you may discover and activate it for yourself. Again, it is not a question of your religion, or lack of it. Healing power is constant. It is neither limited nor increased by labels or associations of any kind. You, too, can do this work.

One man sees a plane above an isolated hut and calls it a miracle. The man in the plane, however, looks at his schedule, checks his instruments, and marks his charts as he flies to New York, and calls it his work. There is no difference in the event, only a difference in the knowledge, understanding and awareness of the laws involved.

It is so easy to speak of miracles and to think of them as something which transcends all law, but the point to remember is that what we call miracles transcend only what we *know* of law. The so-called miracle of your healing depends not upon some supernatural intervention, but only upon what, until now, has been a super-normal experience. When you ask for miracles, then, you ask only for that which is not normal in your experience.

So many pray for miracles, when all that is needed is acceptance of the truth that what they want may be beyond *their normal experience* but not beyond the power of God, of the Infinite Intelligence in them. Why should it be a miracle, why should it involve some supernatural phenomenon for any of us to be healed of illness? Isn't that which created us equally versed in making us whole? Isn't the power which created the planets in such abundance equally capable of directing abundance to us? Isn't the Power that sends blood through the veins —the mysterious surge of life working through law—equal to the task of love? How much some of us trust that which we know, and mistrust that which we do not understand! The man who says, "I'll believe it when I see it," not only refuses to believe in miracles, but has the indescribable ego to judge the unlimited Infinite on the basis of his own limited knowledge and understanding. "Greater works" he will never do.

### How to Achieve Your Miracle

Here is the secret without which the victory, or the "miracle," may not occur: for a moment, an hour, a day or a month, for a year or a lifetime, that which you want, yet which has not been normal for you, must become normal for you. It must, at the precise time you need it, seem and be expected as completely normal and inevitable. For instance, no matter how much or for how long Arnold Palmer worries about his game, feels he might lose, fears his opponents, or doubts his ability, during the game itself he seeks to achieve and maintain an attitude in which winning is completely normal and predictable. For the extent of the tournament, he must throw out everything in his thinking that says it is not right and natural for him to win. It is the one demand inherent in the Law of the Normal Standard.

*For a flashing second or for a lifetime, you must transcend the old normals to which you have grown accustomed, and set new ones in which you believe.* The miracles you see, hear about, or experience, are the direct result of someone's belief; the establishment in mind of a new normal, fleeting and solitary though it may be.

### The Miracle of Frank Eddleston

Frank Eddleston was in a business where he used his voice constantly in interviews, sales meetings, and over the telephone. One day, under the mounting pressures of his life, he suddenly lost his voice. Nothing he did would bring it back. The doctor said, "Don't even try to talk." Months went by. He couldn't utter a word. His secretary had to monitor all his calls, and transmit the messages and their answers. He bought a self-erasing scratch pad in order to communicate with others in writing.

During this time, his 83-year-old mother, who had been blind and deaf for many years, became so critically ill that she was sent to the hospital. One evening not long afterward he received a call that his mother was dying. Immediately he went to see her. He sat quietly by the bed. As she had for many years, his mother ran her hands over his face. Conversation was useless— he couldn't talk, she couldn't hear. Finally, near midnight, he was told that he might as well go home; the end could come at any moment, or it might take several hours.

For a long time he sat in his car in the parking lot outside the hospital. He wanted so much to be able to speak to his mother, to have some kind of verbal communication they had been denied so long. As he sat and thought about it, the intensity of his desire increased. It seemed there was nothing else in life he wanted so much as to speak to his mother, to know that she heard him. As his feelings mounted, Frank prayed. At that moment something happened. He was not sure what it was, but he had a compelling urge to go back into the hospital and see his mother. It was one o'clock in the morning.

He got out of his car, and went back to his mother's room. As he pushed open the door he saw that she was awake. She was looking at him.

"Come in Frank; I was expecting you," she said.

They talked for the next two hours. For the first time in nine months he was able to speak. For the first time in many years, she not only saw him, but heard every word he said. When they had said what seemed necessary to say, and the mother was tired from her exertion, Frank went home. It was three months before he spoke again.

What happened to Frank and his mother? A miracle? Well,

we could use the term. But I believe that what happened was just what we have been discussing. For that brief time between midnight and morning, fired by the intensity of love and the drama of life and death, these two completely forgot their limitations. They became absolutely certain that they could speak, see, and hear. Not once, under the impact of the great emotion which enfolded them, did the thought enter their minds that because they had not been able to speak, see or hear in the past, they could not do it now. There was not the slightest doubt, the weakest fear, the faintest hesitation. In two emotion- and belief-charged hours, it was perfectly normal for them to do just what they did. So they did it!

The next morning when reason set in, when Frank realized that it was not normal for him to be speaking, he became mute again. Not until three more months did he finally overcome his illness. It was not long after that strange night at the hospital that, deaf and sightless once more, his mother left this level of life.

Yes, the so-called "miraculous" can happen when—for an instant, an hour, a day, a week, a month, a year, or a lifetime— you can change your normal expectancy of life, when you can say, accept, and believe of that great dream, of that urgent need, of that deep desire, "this is right, this is normal, this is inevitable for me."

### You Are an Inseparable Part of Miraculous Power

Every person is an extension of Infinite Power. We are not created out of some selfish, cosmic desire, and, once created, tossed upon this earth and forgotten. We are not, and cannot, be separated from that which created us. We are an indivisible part of the One, Perfect Whole, even though we may express that Infinite perfection on a personal, individual basis. What- ever lies within the power of the Infinite is within reach of our powers. What the Infinite created and commands upon a universal, cosmic scale, we create and command upon our own individual, personal scale. We create our own worlds, but we do not create them in powerlessness. We do so with an Infinite power flowing through us. How well we understand and use that power determines how well we fashion a life that is harmonious, happy, beautiful, successful, and healthy.

It is easy for us to believe that in God there is no illness, no weakness, no limitation. It is not always so easy to believe that we, too, may be immune to these human failings. But what is normal to God can be normal to each one of us. We are in the small what God is in the large. We become less than the image of God in us by allowing ourselves to sink to levels of weakness, limitation, helplessness, and despair.

## The True Normal That Is Right for You

*The true normal for each one of us is exactly that which is normal to God*—beauty (whatever the apparent physical appearance may be), love, abundance, health, success, peace, harmony, joy. These are the normals we must accept and in which we must believe for ourselves. These are the normals which belong to us, but which we so often give up because of our limited beliefs.

If your life is an expression of normals less than these, then you must throw out the old normals and create new ones. Do not bind your life to normals that are not worthy of that image of God within you. Illness, and all its causes, are outside the normals of God, and therefore should be outside the normals of man. The consciousness, for instance, that accepts the idea that just because it is Spring it is normal for the body to be subject to epidemics of colds and flu, must be overhauled. The carbon of negative thinking must be cleaned out. Life is choking on the sludge of negative normals. The image of God is distorted and weakened by the imperfect pictures accepted in the human consciousness.

### What to Do When Only a Miracle Will Help

Do you still cling to your old normal complaint that, in your predicament, "only a miracle will help"?

Then turn to the real normals within you.

Turn to the truth that as you are an extension of the one Perfect Presence of the Universe, so you reflect the completeness and perfection of that Presence.

Refuse to despair. Refuse to give up.

Reject any idea that resignation, hopelessness, or self-pity are for you.

Practice the realization of the true normals of beauty, love, abundance, health, success, peace, harmony, and joy within you.

Through a study and application of the principles outlined here, lift your thinking to those levels where you are aware of the power within you to make you well.

### The "Hereness" of Your Healing

As day by day, hour by hour, moment by moment you raise your belief to the point where—even for an instant—that which you want becomes normal for you, you are coming closer and closer to that thrilling instant when healing will be yours. Continue from this moment on to live in the consciousness not of the "thereness" of the healing you want, but of its *hereness.*

Begin your first new normal *now* by putting those healing ideas into *action:*

-------------------------------------------------------------

**EVENING**

*I know that life responds to the normals I set for myself.*
*Tonight I throw out all of the old, unworthy, limited normals that I have accepted for myself in the past.*

No longer is it normal for me to be ill, tired, hurt, beaten, or
defeated.

Tonight life begins to respond to the wonderful normals of
health, strength, happiness, and victory.

## MORNING

A whole day of new, wonderful normals is waiting for me.
This will be a miraculous day.

I am ready to see and accept everything good as normal for
me.

I am now and always part of a miraculous healing power.

My healing is here and now.

## DAY

Today it is impossible for me to fail.

Nothing can keep me from my goal.

I reflect nothing in me but the perfect pattern of health.

There are no substitutes in life.

Healing and health are the natural, normal, expected conditions for me.

I believe in a whole new set of good, happy, successful normals for me.

# 9

## How to Diagnose and
## Heal Minor Health Hazards

There are 8,000 different human ailments, and more than 500 different causes of death. No other living creature suffers more variety in its illnesses than man, and no other living creature faces so many threats to his health and life.

Why is man the sickest of all this world's creatures? Because he thinks!

Health is natural and normal. Illness is unnatural and abnormal. When man falls out of harmony with the laws of his own being, he becomes ill. When he maintains harmony with the laws of his own being, he remains well.

### Avoid the Breaking-Points of Life

Imagine that you are tuning the *D* string on a violin. You try to make it into an *E*, so you tighten it more and more, until it breaks. Someone might ask, "Was it a poor string?" No; it was a good string, but it was the victim of poor tuning. It was not the weakness of the string, but ignorance of the laws of the string that broke it. Was there a weak spot in it? Perhaps. But it was strong enough if it hadn't been stretched beyond the point of its own intrinsic endurance. It would have been good for many hours of beautiful music.

Everyone and every body has some potentially weak point or points. But without undue physical, mental, and emotional strains—without unnecessary stresses, pressures, and loads—they may enjoy a full term of natural life-harmony.

What causes their snapping, their breaking down? Ignorance of the simple laws of body and mind, or failure to live in harmony with those laws. The weakness is not in the body. It is in the mind that tunes it. It is ignorance, or chronic failure to use what one knows that needs to be corrected if the body is not to be stretched beyond its ultimate points of endurance.

Harmony between man and the laws of his own being is disrupted dangerously when there is any serious or sustained conflict between what he believes to be good and evil, between desire and desire, motive and motive, ambition and conscience, emotion and emotion.

This chapter will explain what these conflicts are, what they do to the body, how they can be avoided, and how to heal the results that already may be apparent from them. This will be done by pointing out the causes behind our illnesses, and giving some specific remedies for those causes. It is useless to cut out or dose an effect if the cause of that effect is not eliminated at the same time.

### Understanding the Difference Between Hypochondriacs and the Really Ill

Among the twenty million American men and women who consult a physician every week, there are hypochondriacs (those who suffer from something they do not have), and the really ill (those who suffer from something they do have). The hypochondriac imagines he is ill in his body, when he is ill only in his mind. The body simply reflects the feeling that the mind creates. The ill person, however, actually has some physiological ailment that can be diagnosed, found, and treated. Yet the causes of the false illness and the causes of the true illness may be found in exactly the same place—the mind of the one who is suffering.

To heal either one, then, we must find the often hidden cause in the mind, and heal that. This is not always as easy to do in the case of the hypochondriac, for usually he has a strong belief in the illness he doesn't have, a secret motive for keeping it, and a little pride in his right and opportunity to complain. Also, he is likely to resent the implication that he, and not his body, is ill. He clings to his imagined illness in order to prove that he was right all along. On his tombstone he might approve of that mythical last-word inscription: "See—I told you so!"

In 1962, a court in Sydney, Australia, awarded a woman $25 a week as compensation for a pain which the court agreed was imaginary. The woman claimed that an injury during her work at a certain factory in 1960 caused her persistent pain. Doctors could find nothing physically wrong, yet they testified that she was suffering intensely from an imaginary ailment, and deserved the compensation.

## CAUSATIVE THOUGHTS AND CAUSATIVE THINGS

It is time to repeat one of the most important concepts of this book:

1. The primary cause of everything that happens to us is in the mind. There is always a primary cause. Nothing ever "just happens." There are no accidents; there are only consequences.

2. Usually, but not always, there is a secondary cause. The secondary cause—the one which most often gets blamed for our illnesses—is in, and is a product of, the physical world around us.

There are causative thoughts (primary), and there are causative things (secondary). Causative thoughts always are present. Causative things may be present.

Imagine a room in which the furniture is dusty, while the air itself is clear. Suddenly, a breeze sweeps through the room and swirls the dust about so that the air no longer is clear. The dust was present in the room, but it was not infecting the air until an unrelated disturbance—the sudden breeze—activated it. Viruses and bacteria are like the dust motes. They may be present, yet causing no difficulty in the body, until some unrelated disturbance such as an emotional upset sweeps through the mind and activates them. Viruses or bacteria may have infected a body, but something else is needed to instigate the disease. That "something else," actually unrelated to the virus or bacteria, is *thought*. A person does not get a disease if viruses and bacteria are not present in his body, but neither does he get it simply because viruses or bacteria *are* present in his body.

Physical or emotional disturbances activate the human body's latent cache of germs or viruses which otherwise would remain latent and unharmful. "It's more important," someone once said, "to know what kind of a fella has a germ, than what kind of a germ has a fella."

## To Heal You Must Deal with Causative Thoughts

The purely physical or medical approach to healing is to deal with the causative things, if they are present. This, however, is concerned only with the secondary cause. Consequently, the doctor is often puzzled, or has nothing to treat if the secondary cause is missing. In this case he is apt to give a sugar-pill, a placebo, or to prescribe something that will give only relief.

The mental-emotional-spiritual approach to healing is to deal with the causative thoughts, the primary causes which are always present. Because it contains the originating factors of illness, this is the only area in which true healing can take place.

The world is full of secondary causes. The mind is full of primary causes.

When a person is concerned about which virus, bacteria, or physical deficiency is causing an illness, he is getting into the medical aspects of healing. When he attempts to discover the cause in a person's thinking that has allowed something to express itself in him physically, he is dealing with the mental-emotional-spiritual aspects of healing.

Both are scientific approaches. One is that of the science of medicine; the other is that of the science of mind. But the first—medical science—searching the body, seeks to find and eliminate only the secondary cause; while the second—the science of mind—searching the mind, seeks to find and eliminate the primary cause. While both are valuable in treating illness, medical science (searching the body) can never satisfactorily and completely heal the patient, because it does not eliminate the primary cause; whereas the second, science of mind (searching the mind, using the mental-emotional-spiritual approach), if raised to its highest level, heals the patient and makes the first approach unnecessary.

It becomes increasingly obvious, then, that to maintain harmony in the body, harmony in the mind must also be maintained.

### How to Find the Real Cause

We may ask the question, "What killed Henry?" and receive the answer, "Cirrhosis of the liver." But this is only part of the answer. Getting closer to the truth, we may find that it was over-indulgence in alcohol that brought on the liver ailment. Finally we get to the real truth when we ask, "What caused Henry to drink?" and receive the answer, "He felt inadequate and insecure; liquor helped him forget it."

There, then, we have it—two causative things: over-indulgence in alcohol, and cirrhosis of the liver; and two causative thoughts: inadequacy and insecurity. Without the causative thoughts there would have no effects of, or reason for, the causative things. The causative things were only the agents that, consciously or unconsciously, Henry used to blot out his emotional problem—first, temporarily and spasmodically; second, finally and permanently. This is a simplified example, but every one, simple or complex, begins with a causative thought.

## Some Destructive Primary Causes

To help you recognize the major divisions and some of the specific examples of destructive primary causes, the following summary is given in advance of more detailed discussion.

    I. Emotions—(almost all destructive ones stem from *fear*)
        A. *Stress* emotions:
            A feeling of overload—burdens "too great"
            Too little time—deadline pressures
            Too little money—financial pressures
            A sense of being in the wrong place
            A belief in wrong timing
            Worry and anxiety—specific problem or problems
            Discouragement
        B. *Reaction* emotions (reactions to others):
            Irritation
            Resentment
            Anger—rage
            Hatred—hostility
            Prejudice
            Fear of being hurt, neglected, ignored, rejected, beaten, ridiculed, criticized, destroyed
            Resistance to authority
            Protest
            Impatience
            The feeling of being "trapped"

        Jealousy
        Desire for vengeance
        Habitual embarrassment

   C.  *Reaction* emotions (reactions to one's self)
        Irritation
        Impatience
        Loss
        Grief (sustained)
        Inferiority
        Insecurity
        Inadequacy
        Regret (sustained)
        Resignation to one's failure
        Confusion
        Guilt—need for self-punishment, atonement
                —need or desire to "forget" the error ("crime")
                —need to cover up, hide, or camouflage the error

II.  Thought-Habits or Patterns:
    Spiritual uncertainty
    Indecisiveness—procrastination
    Laziness
    Good beginner—poor finisher
    Diffused anxiety
    Reluctance to change mind or attitude
    Rigidity
    Congenital lying
    Selfishness
    "Me first" attitude
    Expectation and acceptance of unwanted conditions
       (flu, colds, hayfever, epidemics)

III.  Beliefs:
    A belief in fate, chance, destiny, luck—that one has little,
       if any, control over his own experiences
    Superstitions—power of other things over life

The "worst"
Innate unworthiness and selfishness of man (self)
Obstruction or delay
Incompleteness
IV.  Motivations (used harmfully):
Desire for response from others:
Attention
Love
Honor
Respect
Fear
Servitude (obsequiousness)
Motivated by need:
to prove one can succeed
to prove one can fail
(if he *wants* to—
resistance to authority)
to escape
to sacrifice
to "forget":
—not notice
—close off one's awareness
—fail to see or hear
Need to prove one's self:
strong or weak
beautiful or homely
smart or dull
heroic or cowardly
ignorant or intelligent
eccentric or average (normal)
Perfectionism (sense of failure without it)
Fascination with the past
Fascination with suffering and pain
Sadism (compulsion to hurt)

      Masochism (compulsion to be hurt)

      Chronic lying

V. Response to One's Environment (or lack of it):

      Warped or wrong perspectives

      Sensitivity (hurt feelings), pride

      Indifference—lack of interest, apathy, boredom

      Loneliness (brooded upon)

      Stubbornness, bullheadedness, persistent obstinacy

      Desire for quiet, noise, speed, etc. with no other motivation behind it. "I like it."

      Mountain—"Why climb?" "Because it's there."

      Desire for change for change's sake: revolutionaries, crusaders, "Aginners"

      Satisfaction with status quo

        no change, regardless

        comfortable in routine

      The will to fail (ultimate—the will to die)

      Lack of purpose or goal

      Lack of challenge

VI. Phobias (all based on fear, usually childhood shock or experience)

      Fear—space or time locations:

        heights, closed places, dark places, bright places, etc.

        objects

        dirt

        certain animals or insects

        words

Each of the above primary causes, even though the associated needs and motives may have been noble to begin with, have been applied destructively; that is, to the end that the person employing or applying them has become ill. Each possesses the potential emotional content that gives it the power to reflect itself harmfully in the body of the one who harbors it.

### Your Emotions Are the Clues to the Cause

Think of a man who is unemotional, or at least of one who keeps his emotions under perfect control. He has no fears, worries or anxieties; he has no irritations, no jealousies, no resentments, no phobias. He never gets angry, never feels blue, despondent, depressed, or impatient.

Who is this man? He is a figment of the imagination. He doesn't exist. All of us have emotions. Some are good, some are not so good, and some are bad. Some are constructive, some destructive. It is the stresses of life, strung together on the chain of our emotions, which break down and shorten life.

How do you feel about something? This is your emotion, therefore your stress. It may be strong, mild, or weak. It may be quiet, steady, and soothing. It may be intense and explosive. The value or destructiveness of your experiences is not found in what happens, but in how you feel about, or react to what happens.

What motivates or moves you? What is important to you? You have emotions only about that which is important to you.

The Wall Street bull is happy with a continuously rising market, while the bear is unhappy, worried and depressed. Reverse the situation and the emotions are reversed. Again, the emotion depends upon what motivates the man who has it.

An infant is more emotional than we sometimes realize. It already has a sense of values; already there are things which are important to it. It expresses anger, fear, impatience, irritation, annoyance. (Try delaying its feeding for half an hour!) It expresses satisfaction and happiness. It responds to love and attention, as well as to rejection or lack of attention.

The infant eventually becomes the man, and in the process his emotions become mixed and complex; they become his daily companions. They heal him and keep him whole, they make him ill, or they kill him. The emotions of love, joy, happiness, satisfaction, and others like them have brought men and women back from the edge of death, while loneliness, boredom, hatred, anger, jealousy, and others of their kind have caused more deaths than many of the so-called "great killers." Yet, because they cannot be described as physical things, these causes never are recorded on death certificates.

The infant grows into the child, the child into the youth, the youth into an adult. Throughout this time he must, for his own sake, develop the realization that he is carrying in his thoughts a powerhouse of emotion, a powerhouse that must be controlled—not turned off, shut down or stamped out—but controlled, guided, directed, and used.

The man who has always suppressed his emotions is a sick man. His world is sick as well.

It isn't that we should feel guilty because we have emotions, but that we should learn to adjust ourselves to life so that our emotions are neither suppressed, nor allowed to go uncontrolled. The conclusion of a seven year Cornell Medical Center study, reported at a meeting of the American College of Physicians in New York, was that "At least one-third of all man's illnesses, from the common cold to cancer, may now be traced scientifically to the patient's environment, and how well he adapts to it."

### Do Not Fight Your Environment

Your environment is mental as well as physical. Do not fight your environment, but learn to better it, and to help yourself fit happily into it. An emotional reaction to your environment can be either constructive or destructive. Like the stresses in a good bridge, emotions can help hold your personality together. Built into the bridge, however, and built into your personality, must be the devices for making the stresses constructive, rather than destructive.

For every big thing that is important to you, more than likely there are a hundred little ones. For the most part, it is the little things that determine your emotions. It is "the little foxes that spoil the vines." Every day you are faced with the small experiences that can be the basis of a destructive emotion:

how a store clerk responds to your demand for quick service;

how another driver acts on the stretch of road you think ought to be yours;

how someone in the office reacts (or fails to react) to you;

how you do in some task or project;

whether someone writes to you just when you think he should;

whether someone is late for an appointment.

How important, really, are any of these things in relation to the over-all conduct and enjoyment of your life? They would prove to be only small islands of incidentals, having no great value of themselves. Your reaction to them, then, should be one of either quiet observation, helpfulness, or indifference, rather than stressful opposition.

### Don't Let Small Things Become Big Enough to Kill

The giant redwoods are not the only trees which give us apt parallels to the lives we live. For instance, not long ago I read an article about a huge tree on Long's Peak in the Rockies. When Columbus discovered the New World it was a sapling; it was 300 years old when the Declaration of Independence was signed. Fourteen times lightning had struck it, but always it had survived. In its lifetime it had been lashed by high winds and heavy storms, scorched by fire, and scarred by avalanches. For more than 400 years it successfully met each of these challenges. But it fell at last, not to any of these great forces that had been hurled against it for so long, but to countless tiny beetles which had penetrated its trunk and reduced its heart to dust.

We are awed by force and bulk. At time of war we think of

the big guns, tremendous armies, tanks, ever larger and larger ships and submarines, the terrific power of new bombs and explosives. We are fascinated by size, mass, and weight. But every army depends for success on the efficiency of its logistics, its attention to infinite detail, even the seemingly insignificant things. All contribute to the big push, the final offensive that conquers and destroys. Of what use are the great guns without the supply lines? One by one the heavy shells are passed along for the massive bombardment to come later. Of what use would have been the millions of men of World War II without the K-rations (despised as they were), the drab canteens that held the precious water, the mail, and the thousands upon thousands of other details? Without these minutiae, brought to the front by the supply-lines, the big guns would have stood useless, the men would have become weakened and starved; morale would have collapsed; the armies would have disintegrated. Even in the age of the super bomb, attention to infinite detail is needed. Men make small parts, fabricating pieces without knowledge of how or why or where they are to be used. Eventually, however, they fit into the final destructive pattern and purpose of "the Bomb."

The tree on Long's Peak was able to meet and overcome the major challenges, but it succumbed to the little ones. An army at our borders, threatening to destroy us, and able to do so, would still depend upon the smallest details for its destructive power. Remove these, disrupt its logistics, and its destructive power would be gone.

Man sometimes is like the tree. When the major challenges confront him, when the big threats to his security loom ahead of him, he meets them strongly and successfully. He studies the latest methods and products of his particular business. He watches his diet. He gets an adequate amount of exercise and rest. He meets the slow seasons, competition, environment, crises, and changing conditions. But he succumbs to the "beetles" in his thinking—the small, but destructive ideas and emotions which finally do what the great storms of life could never accomplish.

### Don't Make Your Body a Battleground

Your mind possesses the power to heal you, or to destroy you. Socrates said that "in every man is the seed of his own destruction." Through the power of your own mind you can make your body a battleground—a place of suffering, pain, illness, and disintegration. But in your life, the final big push, the ultimate explosion, the great offensive, will often depend for its effectiveness and finality on your supply of seemingly insignificant ideas, beliefs, and emotions.

Many men, giants in business, become ulcerated wrecks because of the persistence of small anxieties supplying the destructive power within them—the little emotional habits that burn up cells, clog the arteries, and unbalance the glands. Many women, careful of their diet, taking nothing but balanced food, and knowing the value of every calorie and protein they consume, nevertheless throw poisons into their systems by their petty jealousies and minor irritations.

Such men and women figuratively have built Maginot lines, battlements of Troy, and walls of China by dedicating certain areas of their time and thinking to physical protection. But they fail to remember that as the real Maginot line was skirted and over-run, as the battlements of Troy were made useless by treachery and stealth, as the walls of China were no protection against the inner conflict of the Chinese war lords themselves, so their physical protections alone are useless and ineffective against the very real destructive mental and emotional forces within themselves.

Watch the little *words* also, for they often represent the emotional level of the mind which uses them. Small, seemingly insignificant words may supply the great explosions of life.

## A Man Who Spoke His Word—
## But Left Out the Right Word

A man I once counselled said that when he was in military service in Florida he vowed that the day he got out he was going to spend two months in bed. The day he was released he was caught between a truck and a trailer and spent the next two months—to the day—in bed. He almost lost his legs. First, both of them were going to be amputated; then one; and finally it was decided to leave them both. He was told, however, that he would never walk again. At one time the ward boy came to look at him, expecting to pull the sheet over his head. "I told him to get a big book," the man said, "and start reading, because he wouldn't have anything else to do for a long, long time."

Here was a man who had the will to live. His faith helped him win the battle of his body. But why was that faith necessary? Why was he called upon to face a crisis which tested and demanded his whole capacity for faith? Why should he have suffered pain and threatened tragedy? Because he failed to realize the significance of so-called "insignificant" words. They were such little things. But they were part of the supply lines for the battle of his body. He spoke his word. The words were formed in his mind. He thought of them. He earnestly desired and believed what he wanted to do. He pictured, imagined, visualized himself just doing nothing for a couple of months. As he visualized, he identified himself with the vision; as he identified himself with it, he accepted it; and as he accepted it, he experienced it. Through the effect of only small thoughts, he was compelled to exercise tremendous faith, not only to keep his legs, but even to stay alive.

If you are to claim any such vision for yourself, be sure to add: "This will come about in the right way for me." If you have power to attract an experience, you also have power to make that experience right for you.

### The Man Who Would "Give Anything . . ."

Another man told me that in a divorce action his wife was awarded $600. He was bitter and resentful. "I'd give anything, anything," he said, "not to pay that $600." In an accident which followed soon after, he lost an eye, and suffered a brain injury. His wife's attorney told him to forget the $600. Irritation, resentment, bitterness, and the words which they called up, were the supply lines for his physical experience. His willingness to give anything made it possible for that "anything" to be *wrong* for *him.*

### Say What You Want, Not What You Don't Want

If you want to avoid such experiences, watch carefully the words you use—say what you want, not what you don't want. Cut off the supply lines that furnish the power of a destructive thought in any way. Your explosive, destructive power will disintegrate when you refuse to feed it your fears, your prejudices, your beliefs or negative emotions, just as the army disintegrates when its supply lines break down, just as no bomb could explode without the attention to the minute details that go into its manufacture.

It doesn't take much insight to realize the truth that man often is a strange creature. He changes nature rapidly. He becomes different persons in different circumstances. His sense of values in one area of life is completely different when applied to another. Many can remember in childhood when they regularly beat up a younger brother, but were Sir-Galahad-to-the-rescue when someone else tried it with that brother. Many men have given their lives for their country, when, in other times, they never even took the time to vote. Many vigorously defend their wives when any reflections are cast upon them, at the same time reserving for themselves the right to criticize, belittle, abuse and sometimes physically punish them. There are those who resent, even fight the efforts of others to block, beat, hurt, criticize, condemn and destroy them, when they are doing all of these things to themselves.

The illnesses we suffer today—attributed though they may be to manifestations of the physical world, and called by the names of medicine—are created, supplied, maintained and supported by emotions and attitudes which we often ignore because they are so common. Anger, jealousy, hate, resentment, bitterness, regret, worry, anxiety and fear. These are among the negative emotions and beliefs with which we afflict ourselves. They are joined by those created when we believe, imagine, identify ourselves with, or accept that which we are afraid of, or do not want. These are sometimes the overlooked or so-called "forgotten" thoughts and words upon whose patterns the mind creates our experiences. We may do what we wish to fight the effect, but unless we eliminate the cause, the effect will continue.

A news story some time ago told of a man who, in a burst of emotion, shot a motion-picture screen full of holes. It didn't stop the picture. Unless we do something to eliminate the causes of our illnesses, we can shoot the body full of holes, too (hypodermically speaking), but the effects will continue just the same.

So it is that our bodies become battlegrounds—battlefields subject to minor skirmishes of colds, sinus, hay-fever, headaches, and dizziness; constantly alerted to the recurrent raids of broken bones, exzema, accidents and loss, while the medicine-chest becomes an arsenal of anti-bacteria bombs. Occasionally the conflict becomes major, and our bodies reel under arthritis, paralysis, failing eyesight, impaired hearing, physical breakdowns and deterioration. They become locked in decisive battles with man's most destructive diseases in which the very preservation of the body is at stake.

## Where Can the Body Find Peace?

What can we do that will bring peace to this battle-scarred physical thing that we call our body? The first step is to cut off that which supplies the weapons for the conflicts—the negative ideas and beliefs, the words and thoughts which contain a negative emotion. It is then that the armies of destruction begin to die on the vine.

But this is not always enough. If it were, this book would end right here. For an instantaneous, complete, and permanent healing to take place, we must discover all the secrets of this book, one by one, and then conscientiously apply them to life.

## You Are in Command

No one can eliminate the destructive emotions for you. You must do it for yourself. No one but you can disrupt the logistics of your destructive thought-process. You are in command of your own mind. You are the one who can determine whether it is building for battle, or building for peace.

If you intend to be building for peace, then it is time now to cut off the supply of worry, irritation, bitterness, jealousy, anger—all the negative ideas, thoughts and emotions that build the disrupting experiences in life. It is time now to build *into* your mind a quiet confidence and faith. It is time now to acquire the habit of constructive thinking even in the smallest things, for even the smallest creative, harmonious thought will begin adding its healing power to every area and activity of your life.

All during this night and the coming day put these healing ideas into *action:*

## EVENING

*Tonight an infinite calm settles over my mind.*

*I turn my thoughts to whatever things of beauty and peace I like to think of.*

*I rest my thoughts on these things. I will not be moved by anything but the desirable and the good.*

*My dreams tonight shall be dreams of pleasantness.*

## MORNING

*I am ready to be moved to joy today.*

*I look forward to wonderful, healing experiences throughout this day.*

*Today I shall think only positive things, for in my thoughts I know I create the causes of my life.*

## DAY

*Today I think only of what I want. I do not think of what I do not want.*

*Today I do not say or claim anything I do not want to see come true.*

*I watch every word. My body, my mind, my whole being is a place of peace.*

*Everything happens in the right way for me.*

*I am in command of every moment of my life.*

# 10

## How to Recognize, Root Out, and Eradicate the Six Major Health Wreckers in Your Life

Your emotions, attitudes, and beliefs are like a deck of cards. Individually, they can be counted and catalogued. But in combinations they can be multiplied by the thousands. Only a few, however, are responsible for the major damages to your health, and it is these dangerous few I want to point out to you now.

They are so common as to be responsible for almost every illness or difficulty of life. Because they are so common, we sometimes have the tendency to underestimate them. If you want to be healed of any illness, whether you consider it major or minor, study this list of emotions, attitudes, and beliefs carefully; then study yourself to determine whether any of these primary causes apply to you.

I will give the basic word or group of words that tells what the primary cause may be; a short explanation of that primary cause; occasional examples showing possible results of allowing it to go unchanged or unchecked; some healing truths, and the new attitudes or beliefs that will eliminate it.

Several of these primary causes of illness and disease are

mentioned elsewhere in this book. Here, however, you will find a simple summary of each one to help you trace, recognize, and overcome them in your own life.

## 1. Irritation

*The underlying attitude or belief:* Someone or something has the power to irritate you without your consent, making you react "automatically," "instinctively," "normally," "naturally."

Among the illnesses and diseases that may be traced to irritation are these: (Notice the prevalence of those ending in *-itis*)

| | |
|---|---|
| colitis | shingles |
| gastritis | hives |
| tonsillitis | cold sores |
| laryngitis | hay fever |
| sinusitis | asthma |
| neuritis | allergies |
| itching | indigestion |
| eczema | skin rashes and diseases |

*The Healing Truths:*

1. You cannot be irritated by anything without your consent.

2. Nothing has any power of itself to irritate you that you do not *give* it. No one has any power to irritate you that you do not *give* him or her.

3. You are irritated by your *reaction* to something or someone, *not* by the someone or the something itself. (What irritates one may not irritate another.) The Hottentot says: "Good is when I steal other men's wives and cattle; bad is when they steal mine."

(To repeat Marcus Aurelius: "If you are pained by any external thing, it is not this that disturbs you, but your own judgment about it.")

4. When you accept your irritation as "automatic," "instinctive," "normal," or "natural" you are admitting that you do not have control over your own emotions. In effect you blame them

on inborn tendencies that you have refused to discipline. This is the mark of the emotionally immature who threaten to become the physically sick.

5. You give other persons or conditions the power to control and dominate you when you allow them to irritate you. They capture and hold your thoughts, and they have power over your body, making the body processes unbalanced—blood rising to the head, voice high-pitched, fingers shaking, reflexes off. Habitual or consistent irritation will lead your entire body to more destructive and more permanent weakness and imbalance.

6. The person who feels inferior or inadequate will often try to irritate you in an effort to bring you down to his level and make his inferiority or inadequacy less noticeable. When you become irritated with him, you are playing *his* game, and immediately you are at a big disadvantage.

*The Healing Attitude or Belief:*

The following statements, and others like them in subsequent chapters, called *Healing Attitudes and Beliefs,* are longer examples of the *Evening, Morning* and *Day* thoughts. They are intended as supplements, not as substitutes for the Idea Cards. Read them as you come to them. Then return to them at any time you feel they meet your special attitude or emotional problem.

I suggest you mark these also with a slip of paper so that you can turn to them easily. Do not skip the Idea Cards simply because you have read these. The Idea Cards are your working materials to put these healing secrets into action.

All of these statements are designed to correct the error-habits of your thoughts and emotions, for in these will be found the true primary causes of your illnesses. In your corrected thoughts and emotions will also be found the key to your true healing.

*Note:* You have been using this type of mental treatment each evening, morning, and day. It is not, as some might have supposed, a type of self-hypnosis. Its purpose is to unite your consciousness with the healing, creative principles of life, and to retrain and redirect your subconscious thought-patterns and habit-patterns into agreement. It places you in conscious touch with Infinite Power. It gives you an operating base, so to speak, from which you can change both your conscious and subconscious state of mind from the destructive (which attracts illness) to the constructive (which attracts healing and health). We do not "go out after" either illness or health. By our destructive or constructive (negative or positive) states of mind, we simply make ourselves receptive to illness or health. Mental treatment, then, is the most effective method of making yourself receptive to whatever you desire.

The healing attitudes or beliefs governing release from irritation are the following:

"I refuse to be irritated by anything or anyone.

"I give nothing and no one the power to irritate me.

"I am at perfect peace within myself because I am part of an Infinite perfection in which there is no irritation.

"I do not try to dominate the thinking and actions of others, but I can and do control my own.

"I may understand the desire or inclination of others to irritate me (office, home, sports, etc.) but I refuse to react. This nullifies their action, and leaves me free of their influence or power."

## 2. Overload

*The underlying attitude or belief:* The pressures and loads of life, circumstances, job, responsibilities, challenges, etc. are too great for you to bear.

"I can't go through with it."

"It's more than I can stand."

"I can't take it any longer."

"I've just got too much to do."

Such attitudes and beliefs are brought on by deadlines, constant pressure for more and better work, no let-up on the volume of work you want or are expected to do, a job condition in which you can't seem to catch up, one in which, no matter how hard you try, you are always behind. In short, goals too difficult to reach, coupled with a feeling that you can't "just quit."

Among the illnesses, difficulties, and diseases that may be traced to overload are these:

| | |
|---|---|
| paralysis | voice defects |
| nervous breakdown | stroke |
| dizziness | rupture |
| varicose veins | tuberculosis |
| swollen ankles | palpitation of the heart |
| neurosis | muscular troubles |
| alcoholism | |

When Roger Maris was making his spectacular try at breaking Babe Ruth's home run record of 60, he was under such pressure from both himself and the fans that his hair began to fall out. The pace and mounting tension were so great that big tufts of hair on the back and on the sides of his head dropped off. A Baltimore doctor assured Maris that it was only "a case of nerves," not some strange disease as he had feared. The doctor told him that the strain had been building and increasing for some time, and that when the big test was over, and he could relax, the hair would grow back again. When the season closed and the pressure was gone, Maris' hair did grow back.

*The Healing Truths:*

1. No person is truly indispensable. Nothing needs you so much that you can afford to make yourself ill, or to kill yourself, in an effort to practice or support it.

2. While you are not specifically indispensable, your health

is indispensable to you if your life is to be effective, efficient, and free from pain.

3. One of your great freedoms is to choose how much you want to do in this world. The pressures you suffer are the pressures you accept.

4. Anything and everything that comes to you is somehow attracted to you because of what you are. It is yours by right of your own consciousness. Therefore, you are prepared in consciousness to handle it, or it wouldn't have come to you.

5. You draw upon an inner strength far greater than you suppose. This strength fails you only when you believe it will fail, or are afraid it will fail. Your capacity for meeting the challenges, pressures and responsibilities of life is far above what you normally think of it as being. You are part of an Infinite strength which will translate itself into your own mental, emotional, or physical strength when you call upon it with quietness and faith.

## Suggestions:

Avoid all feelings of desperation. Desperation merely breeds more desperation.

Know that nothing comes to you that you cannot either handle or change. You do not need to be tied to anything that demands more of you than you want or are prepared to give.

If you feel a sense of overload, start accepting in mind now that time, whenever it may be, when you are in command of both yourself and your work load. If you feel it necessary or advisable, find some other work to do that is more in harmony with your work capacity and work habits. Whatever you do, don't continue day after day under a strain that you *can* change.

If your work and responsibilities are getting greater every day, remember that this may indicate growth—growth of the business and growth of your own consciousness. A business which started out with a few employees may now need a hundred. The few came to the point where they could not handle the increased work. Instead of getting panicky, or a sense of overload, they realized that they needed help because of a healthy increase in business, not because they were slowing down under the load.

Whatever job you have to do, do the best you can, and let it go at that. No one can ask that you do anything better than you can. Try to improve your techniques and facilities, but do not struggle with what you have.

### Healing Attitudes and Beliefs:

"I always have the time and the strength to do that which I want to do, need to do, and that is right for me.

"Whenever any extra load or challenge faces me, I can draw upon an extra supply of inner strength to carry it or meet it. Infinite power flows through me at all times; I am never without it.

"I refuse to feel tension, desperation, undue pressure, or a sense of struggle. I will always get done what *has* to be done for my own good, and for the fulfillment of my responsibilities.

"In everything, I do the best I can, and I know that best will be enough."

### 3. Obstruction and Delay

*The underlying attitude or belief:* Someone or something has the power to block you, or to delay your getting what is good and right for you.

Such an attitude or belief often begins in childhood (for a very good reason) and is carried over into adult life (where there is no reason at all). Children are subject to both discipline and domination, under which they often find themselves unable to get what they want. The parents, or their brothers and sisters, demonstrate a real power to obstruct and delay them, and they begin to believe that others can do this also. The belief of childhood (supported by an abundance of evidence) becomes the belief of their later years (supported only by their own acceptance of such power of others over them).

Promises made to children, and then broken or delayed, lead children to fear disappointment. Time is longer to a child than to an adult, and the delay that seems moderate to a parent may seem an eternity to a child.

When hoped-for, expected, or promised pleasures are indefinitely postponed because the parents say, "We can't afford it," the child is given yet another reason to believe in obstruction and delay.

It makes no difference what the reason may be for your belief in obstruction and delay, how valid it seems to be, or how documented by fact it may become, the belief itself is dangerous. The belief that you can be obstructed or delayed in any area of life can lead not only to illness, but to the obstruction and delay of your healing as well.

Among the illnesses and difficulties that can be traced to obstruction and delay are these:

> indigestion
> hardening of the arteries
> poor circulation
> coronary occlusion

Because the body always tends to express itself in harmony with the mind, the body will reflect the belief in obstruction and delay through the obstruction and delay of the bodily functions and parts. Indigestion, hardening of the arteries, poor circulation, and coronary occlusion all are examples of such failure or breakdown in the body.

*Healing Truths:*

There is no obstruction or delay in the Infinite. Because you are part of that Infinite, you need accept nothing of this in your own individual life.

There is a resistless flow of power moving you toward your chosen goals, provided you do not obstruct or delay yourself by believing or fearing that something can happen to stop or disappoint you.

*Suggestions:*

Stop looking for persons, things or conditions that can hinder you. Stop giving them power over you by your belief in them. Keep looking for those that can give you some constructive help on your way.

Make your choices firm and clear. If they are weak and indecisive, it will be your own weakness and indecisiveness which will stand in your way. Stop tying yourself in knots emotionally, or the body will begin to do the same within itself.

*The Healing Attitude or Belief:*

"I am now moving freely and effortlessly toward my good.

"Nothing has the power to keep my good from me.

"Nothing can obstruct or delay my reaching that state or condition of life I choose.

"There is a resistless circulation of all good things through my life, and this resistless circulation includes my body and all its rightful functions.

"I am making easy, continuous progress toward everything in life I want."

### 4. Wrong Placement

*The underlying attitude or belief:* You are in your wrong place, or something or someone important to you is in the wrong place.

The major feeling is one of dislocation. If you feel this sense of dislocation (of yourself, something, or someone else being in the *wrong* place) your body will begin to reflect some physical counterpart of this mental or emotional state.

For instance, your belief in your being trapped in the wrong job and the physical difficulty of occasionally having your back go out of place may seem to be unrelated, but one is a belief in wrong placement, while the other is its physical reflection. The idea of wrong placement in one thing will operate destructively in another.

A very subtle form of this belief is found in those who are always referring to their childhood towns as "back home." They may have been gone from them for 10, 20, or 30 years, yet they still claim them as home. Because the human consciousness usually places more emphasis and value on "home" than anywhere else, such a claim is a conscious or subconscious admission that one is in his wrong place. Although of very low grade emotionally, this belief begins to have a destructive effect because of the years-long persistence in it. To be safe, accept where you are as "home," even though you know it will be temporary. Do not allow yourself to feel separated from that place which belongs to you, and to which you belong.

Typical of those who believe in wrong placement are those who say, "I'm never in the right place at the right time," or, "I'm always in the right place at the wrong time."

Among the illnesses and conditions that may be traced to wrong placement are these:

> fallen and misplaced organs
> slipped discs
> sacroiliac trouble
> accidents
> losing things
> arthritis (see separate discussion of arthritis on page 185)

### The Healing Attitude or Belief:

> "I am always in my right place at the right time. Everything that is necessary to my happiness and well-being is always in its right place.

"Every cell in my body (as every atom in the universe) is always in its right place.

"Whenever I become dissatisfied with where I am (job, home, city, etc.) it is a divine dissatisfaction, not merely dissatisfaction. This means that I am going to find a better place at the right time for me, and that I am not going to become upset by where I am now."

### 5. Separation

*The underlying attitude or belief:* You can be separated from that which you want, that which is right and good for you.

Among the illnesses and difficulties that may be traced to separation are these:

broken bones
torn ligaments
injured muscles
eye injuries and difficulties
loss of all kinds

Mrs. Lawson felt a deep sense of loss when her brother, who had lived with her for the past 20 years following the death of her husband, also died.

Within the week she fell and broke her arm.

Mrs. Granley felt completely separated from her good when her husband was sent to jail while her son was away in the service.

She slipped on a rug and broke her hip.

Greg Peterson's wife left him for another man. He was distraught. He felt that everything that meant anything to him had been taken from him.

Shortly thereafter he was in an automobile accident in which he lost a leg.

Over a period of years, Mrs. Harding, a widow on pension, constantly feared that her security would somehow be taken away from her, that she would lose her home, and that her relatives would separate themselves from her and leave her alone.

After a long siege of chronic difficulty, she was forced to go to the hospital and have one of her kidneys removed.

(The exact and undeniable connection between these thoughts, beliefs, emotions and fears, and the physical difficulty encountered by these persons and others like them would be difficult to prove. The body is not yet the kind of test tube in which we invariably can watch and prove the relationship between a thought and certain physical conditions. Yet the vast volume of case-histories in my files and the files of others who study and deal with the psychosomatic factors in accidents and illness reveal an unmistakable relationship between thought and body-experience. The proof of any specific case may always be questioned by someone, while the evidence to support this contention in general is too great to be the subject of much doubt.)

*The Healing Attitude or Belief:*

"I can never be separated from my good. No one can take from me that which is rightfully mine.

"I am now and always united with everything I want and need.

"I claim perfect union with life, happiness, wholeness, and the abundantly good."

## 6. Hostility and Cross-Purposes

*The underlying attitude or belief:* You are living in a world hostile to your own needs and desires. Competition is always tough and mean. It's a case of "tooth-and-claw, dog-eat-dog." You have to fight in order to get and keep what you need for your survival. Everybody is against you.

The person who punishes himself with this primary cause believes that there are persons, forces, circumstances, or things which are hostile to and at cross-purposes with his own desires and goals.

Suspicion, doubt, hatred, antagonism, mistrust, and hostility are key words in finding the primary causes behind your troubles.

Among the illnesses, difficulties, and diseases that may be traced to hostility and cross-purposes are these:

anemia
sore throat
pneumonia
hypertension
infections
bacterial diseases
indigestion
cancer

*Anemia* may reflect a person's belief in the absence of cooperation, love, or consideration from the world.

A *sore throat* may be the signal of hostility between a man and his boss, or a man and his wife.

*Pneumonia* sometimes results from a person's long-standing, or sudden and intense belief that circumstances have conspired against him, that the things on which he could depend have turned against him.

*Indigestion* may be the body's way of telling you to forget your anger, to release your suspicions, and to go on about your business in an alert but at the same time relaxed state of mind.

*The Healing Truths:*

The purpose of the Infinite (God) is balance and harmony, supply and adequacy.

When you believe in hostile competition, generalized enmity and antagonism, you furnish the body atmosphere in which bacteria flourish and multiply so rapidly that they exterminate your body—their host—and so themselves. To destroy their host (your body) is not the intention of the bacteria. If the term could be applied to them, we could say they are "happy" to be there. But when you maintain an attitude of hostility, and a belief in cross-purposes, you are making it possible for the bacteria to over-populate themselves in you—a condition which will prove disastrous for both of you.

When you continue such emotional imbalance, you furnish an atmosphere in which it becomes difficult for the bacteria to enjoy you, and not destroy you!

Bacteria will not flourish destructively in an atmosphere into which they have not been "invited." The calm, quiet, loving approach to life—at the same time backed by strong faith and belief in the essential goodness of human nature—will prove to be the greatest mental-spiritual safeguard against any bacterial invasion.

*The Healing Attitudes or Beliefs:*

"I am surrounded by harmony and good-will.

"I dwell in peace, and I am always ready with forgiveness.

"I believe in the essential goodness of human nature, and while I quietly protect myself against the errors in another's thinking, I look past those errors into the true person he is and can be.

"There is no *destructive* competition. I believe in *constructive* competition—that which stimulates me to improve my work or my products, keeps me on my toes, and sees that I do not fall into the habit of taking things for granted.

"I look upon life as a game, not a struggle. What appears to be hostility is only the intensity with which the rest of the world seeks to reach its goals, just as I do mine.

"I consciously create a mental-emotional-spiritual attitude of mind in which only good can prevail, for it is an attitude of confidence, serenity, and peace."

Here are your healing ideas to be put into *action*. Read them and work with them as if they were your own original convictions.

●··●··●··●··●··●··●··●··●··●··●··●··●··●··●··●··●··●··●··●··●··●··●··●··●··●··●··●·

## EVENING

*Tonight I am freeing my mind of every sense of pressure.*
*I am relaxed. Tension falls away from me.*
*I do not think of what happened today. I do not think of what will happen tomorrow.*
*I know only that tonight will be a wonderful time of rest.*

●··●··●··●··●··●··●··●··●··●··●··●··●··●··●··●··●··●··●··●··●··●··●··●··●··●··●··●·

## MORNING

*I am ready to face this day with new and brighter attitudes.*
*I shall watch the great results that my healed attitudes make in me and in those around me.*
*Today I shall create only* healthy *causes.*

●··●··●··●··●··●··●··●··●··●··●··●··●··●··●··●··●··●··●··●··●··●··●··●··●··●··●··●·

## DAY

*Today I refuse to be irritated by anything or anyone.*
*I am adequate. I have all the strength I need to do what I have to do.*
*Nothing can obstruct or delay me.*
*All ways are open to me.*
*I am now and always in my right place.*
*I never can be separated from that which is rightfully mine.*
*I am at peace with myself and my world.*

●··●··●··●··●··●··●··●··●··●··●··●··●··●··●··●··●··●··●··●··●··●··●··●··●··●··●··●·

# 11

# How to Spot and Overcome "Family-Factor" Illnesses

It is a biological fact that the body reaches a state of maturity long before the mind. To put it another way: except in unique instances, the body is able to reproduce itself long before the mind is able to produce consistently mature thoughts. Consequently, the physical ability of the body to reproduce itself precedes the mental, emotional, and spiritual ability of the mind to give such reproductions infallible, or at least adequate protection.

This is why a child which is physically perfect may be born into a family which is mentally, emotionally, and spiritually far from perfect. This is why the physically perfect body may begin to reflect the mental, emotional or spiritual imperfections, errors, and immaturities by which it is surrounded, and into which it is born.

## How a Child Reflects Its Problems

Ordinarily, the child has no mental talent, emotional strength, or spiritual training to protect itself from its environment. As a

151

result, it begins to reflect the destructive influences which may surround it through asthma, eczema, colds, fever, accidents, or stuttering (all on the physical side), and through fear, indecisiveness, nervousness, irritation, hostility, loneliness, inadequacy, and guilt (all on the mental, emotional, and spiritual side).

In most cases, the father and mother are relatively young when a child is born. By their youth they are denied the experience which creates maturity, and they may bring with them —into *their* young married life—the destructive, or at least, the conflict-producing attitudes acquired from their own physically mature, yet mentally, emotionally, and spiritually immature father and mother. Thus, negative influences may be perpetuated from generation to generation, until the consequent results become so routine as to be labeled *family characteristics*.

## How Family Habit-Patterns Affect Your Health

The habit-patterns of immature thought, handed down from family to family, are responsible for many of the tendencies blamed on the genes. That such sickly, immature thinking is allowed to continue presents a sad commentary upon the general attitude of men and women today who:

1. are willing to accept the old patterns of their own family, simply because it was theirs;
2. are unwilling to find and correct the primary cause of their difficulties, preferring to blame them on something "untouchable" or fate-directed "out there"; and,
3. even when forced to accept the great revelations of *physical* science, still prefer to hang on to old superstitions by rejecting the great revelations of *mental* science; and who,
4. when the way to mental, emotional and spiritual maturity is so freely offered and available, choose to ignore it, not only by living the tension-filled, conflict-torn, fear-wracked

existence for themselves, but by infecting the lives of their children with it as well.

Because the child cannot always protect itself, and because it ordinarily will reflect the weaknesses along with the strengths of its family unit until it becomes an independent, self-directed entity, the responsibility of every father and mother is to lead the child to the mental, emotional, and spiritual strengths that their physical strength made necessary and possible. Furthermore, because the mind has its human loopholes through which we allow the misconceptions of our true powers and our true selves to invade our consciousness, each of us has a responsibility to himself to find out what those powers are and who he truly is, and then to live up to these potentials. Jesus put it bluntly when he said, "Think not that I am come to send peace on earth; I came not to send peace, but a sword. For I am come to set a man at variance with his father, and the daughter against her mother, and the daughter-in-law against her mother-in-law. And a man's foes shall be they of his own household." Do not be led into a strictly literal or physical interpretation of this. It speaks of the same things I speak of here, except that it speaks in the terms of symbol and parable. For the truth is that the "family-factor" is at the root of much of our world's illnesses today. This is because we do have:

1. the superstitious, fate-bound attitude toward life,
2. the tendency to react negatively to negative family habits, and
3. a false idea of the demands of love, coupled with a warped idea of the value of sympathy.

There are infinite ramifications to this last one. It is to all three, however, that the "family-factor" applies, and it is to the family-factor as the cause of much of our illness that I call your attention.

### The Family-Factor in Asthma, Eczema, and Throat Infections

There are many primary causes of asthma. Some have their origin in the adult years, but most of them begin in childhood, for in childhood one faces problems and crises that so often seem insurmountable.

Frustration and irritation, among the major primary causes of asthma, may be daily occurrences for one who would like to express himself in his own fashion, yet must conform to family patterns or parental whims.

Asthma may be a violent inward protest against over-indulgence and over-protection, or against rejection—a feeling of being unwanted and unloved. This matter of protest is so common that it will be discussed more completely later in this chapter. (See page 173.)

Unstable emotional conditions in the home may also result in asthmatic attacks in the children. The feeling of a child that never knows what to expect next from his parents—happiness or sorrow, love or hate, solicitousness or indifference, laughter or tears, generosity or stinginess, bickering or pleasantness—makes him retreat into asthma. At least asthma is something upon which, even though it pains him, he can depend.

When a child discovers that he has parents who get hysterical every time he has an attack, and who drop everything to attend to his every wish, he may begin to use his attacks to dominate his parents and to take attention away from his brothers and sisters. In such cases he may prove to be a difficult patient because he really is reluctant to give up this powerful means of family control. (See Chapter 6.) As the illness progresses and as time goes by, the child may suddenly realize that if he were to get well, he would have to do his share of family work, he would have to help around the house and eventually go out into the world and get a job, like his brothers and sisters. By this time he may have developed such a sense of dependence, or such a liking for his place of pampered illness in the family, that again he holds on to his asthma as his protection against having to give up that place and to face life and its demands.

The Jewish National Home for Asthmatic Children in Denver, Colorado is reserved especially for asthmatic children of all faiths. Very little medical treatment is given there. Most of the treatment does nothing more than change the attitude and mental environment of the children. Many cases of chronic, intractable asthma, during which attacks the patients cough, wheeze, gasp for breath, and even come close to dying, are brought to the point where they are completely "controlled." One particular treatment is insisted upon for every child admitted: the absolute separation of the child from its parents and other members of its family. The chief medical consultant calls it "parentectomy." Boys and girls are given a complete change from the home environment, no matter how sympathetic or conscientious the parents may be. It is often that this very sympathy and conscientiousness causes the asthma by its "smothering" effect upon the child. The parents' reactions to the child's problems may cause it to become asthmatic in an effort to gain attention and sympathy.

Many asthmatic children, says the director, have some basic conflict with one or both parents, a conflict which is very serious to the child, although it might seem of no importance to the parents.

In other cases the child feels overwhelmed by some family emotional problem it feels powerless to help or overcome.

For many children asthma becomes a subconscious weapon they use against their parents for some act or failure to act that the children think is unfair or wrong.

When the American Academy of Pediatrics met in Chicago some time ago, an entire symposium was devoted to the "family-factor" in illness. Information coming from the symposium confirmed many of the observations made here. For instance, when a seven year old girl developed eczema on her arm, a pediatrician prescribed salve. An allergist told her to stop eating eggs. Their advice was followed, but the rash continued to spread. Then the girl's mother remarked to one doctor that her husband had been fired from his last job. Immediately, the doctor knew that the household tensions, worry, and fear had reflected themselves physically on the girl's arms. She was put into the hospital where she could be separated from the household emotions. The eczema improved, and finally disappeared.

Dr. Robert J. Haggarty of Harvard Medical School reported that almost any crisis in the family may precipitate a strep throat. The death of a grandparent, moving to another home or school, the illness of a parent, the breaking up of a friendship, bad grades, or difficult school experiences are often the prelude to throat infections. In fact, said Dr. Haggarty, the incidence of strep throat was *preceded* by such occurrences four to one, as against the times when they *followed* such infections. Any family crisis lowers the child's resistance, making it receptive to infection.

### How to Gauge the Emotional Condition of Your Family

Whenever an illness attacks a child, we examine closely the emotional condition of the family that surrounds it, for a child is a reflection of the environment in which it lives. Until boys or girls grow to the age where they can make their own decisions, and have some sense of command over their own circumstances, they are nothing more than extensions of the father and mother. It is the uncontrolled emotions, the lack of mental discipline, and the insecurity of the parent that makes itself known on the physical level in the child. When the parents are healed of their fears, their emotional binges, their irritations and weaknesses, the child usually will be healed as well.

### How to Detect the "Childish"
### Illnesses of Adult Years

Those adults who have carried the illnesses of childhood over into their later years may also conquer the primary causes of these illnesses when they realize that the past circumstances of life no longer are valid or dominating in the present. Illnesses sometimes become habitual, however, and continue even when their primary causes have disappeared. When this happens, the adult must be willing to admit that his illness is caused by something out of the past, and that it has no power to continue hurting him in the present.

There also are those who find other reasons for reacting childishly and destructively to circumstances in these later years. From my files come the following six family-factor examples. (The apparent primary cause or causes are in parentheses.)

Every time a certain woman in X company comes to the office with a cold, you know she has been fighting with her husband. (*Irritation*)

One man was so upset over separation from his wife that he lost 28 pounds, caught pneumonia, and almost died. (*Loneliness, Separation*)

A lawyer dreamed of kicking his father—an act which he devoutly wished to fulfill—and through some "mysterious" ailment, lost the use of his leg for six weeks. (*Guilt*)

A salesman so hated his brother that the hate appeared as a cancer. In his last illness, to which he had come penniless, his brother was put to an almost ruinous expense. (*Hostility* and *Cross-Purposes*)

A certain woman felt so guilty about going away and leaving her mother alone on the day she died, that she began manifesting all the symptoms of her mother's illness. In a little less than three years she went to a sanitarium where she stayed until she, too, died. She had come to see me shortly after her mother's death, but because she so concentrated on her mother's illness, and in the end preferred keeping her sense of guilt, she rejected the help I could have given her. *(Guilt)*

A young bride is so afraid of her in-laws that she gets an upset stomach every Sunday afternoon because her husband might want to go see them, or they might drop by. *(Fear)*

The desire to remain forever a part of one's early family is the primary cause of many other puzzling and persistent illnesses:

A man professes and experiences weakness and timidity in order to remain the protected little boy.

A woman becomes an invalid in order to remain under her childhood roof.

A widow sacrifices every chance to draw some new love into her life because she would rather possess her son than to see him happily married. She builds into his consciousness a sense of debt for what she has "given up" on his account, and subtly turns it into complete dependency upon her for the slightest decision he is called upon to make. Eventually he reaches that ultimate state of emotional immaturity in which even the thought of his going out with women, of marrying one, of fulfilling all the duties of a husband, makes him sick at his stomach. His mother babies him in his every need, and his bad days, when he needs her more than ever, are her days of heaven.

### Seeing the Effects of Guilt and Pain in Family-Factor Illnesses

Guilt, too, deserves special treatment later, but in the family connection it must not be overlooked.

One woman is suffering terrible pains from an illness the doctors can neither diagnose nor treat, because her son died in a hunting accident. It was she who gave him permission to go on the hunting trip. "I should never have done it!" she repeats over and over. He would be here today, she says, if she had just had the good sense to say "No." Now she believes that she, his own mother, should not really enjoy life because her son came to such a tragic end through her own decision. She will not reach any kind of healing until first she realizes that her son could have come to the end of his life anywhere else according to his own consciousness, regardless of any decision she might or might not have made.

When we accept the belief that we somehow are responsible for another's life or death, especially when such an intention was not part of our thoughts at the time, we are assuming a power and a responsibility far beyond that which we truly possess. We are placing ourselves in the position of life-giver, or death-giver, and we have no such power at all. When we do the best we can, and make our decisions in the light of our knowledge and best judgment at the time, we must not perpetuate a sense of guilt, and live in a state of self-condemnation. The blighting of one life cannot repay for the loss of another.

## How Failing Eyesight Was Traced to the Family

A professional woman had fallen under the insidious influence of a father and mother who possessed her with their love. She had stayed home with her father and mother while her brothers and sisters had gone out and made their own lives.

"What will we do if *you* leave?" they asked her plaintively. When she accepted dates, she would come home and find them both ill, neither one able to take care of the other one. They looked at her reproachfully, as if she had been thoughtless to go away and leave them alone.

She was an intelligent woman. She knew what they were doing to her, yet she tried not to see it. She hid from herself the realization that they were strangling her true nature, that they were imprisoning her by means of her own conscience. Her brothers and sisters tried to point out all of this to her, but she would hear nothing of it.

Eventually she began to have serious difficulty with her eyes. Her sight began to dim. Glasses did not help; the oculist could find nothing for which he could prescribe. Yet, little by little it seemed that she was going blind. This was when she came to see me.

When I had heard and analyzed her story, I very carefully brought her to the admission that she was allowing an unfair restriction to be placed upon her own life. She was refusing to "see" what was happening to her life, and therefore, her life was simply following the direction of her mind. By closing off her *inner* sight, she found she was closing off her *outer* sight as well.

The body is an amazing instrument which does everything possible to reflect the mind which controls it. A refusal to see life begins to result in an inability to see what is in and around that life. The body follows the suit of the mind.

This woman and I discussed the family-factor. After several conferences, in which she finally allowed herself to see what her family was doing to her, she made both her decisions and her recovery. She retained her love for her father and mother. She remained willing, even eager to do what she could for them. But at the same time she declared her mental, emotional, and spiritual independence from them. She gave up the role of the little girl, and became the woman. She saw her parents and herself in their true relationship for the first time. It was a vision of clarity. There were no blurs of false emotions and indistinct motives. It was then that her sight began to improve. In a little more than two weeks she was healed. The realization of a moment was reflected in an instantaneous healing of the cause of her difficulty, and the difficulty simply disappeared.

### How a Woman's Deafness Proved to Be Family Connected

I once knew a man and wife who were rather sensitive persons, both artistic and productive. She was quiet; he was highly voluble. Occasionally they talked to each other, but more often than not he just talked to her. He went on endlessly, droning away in his monotonous voice. Hour after hour he talked. Hour after hour she listened, until it became so irritating to her that it reached the point where she wished she could never have to listen to him again.

Thereafter, while answering with little grunts now and then, by nodding her head, or by making some other small act of recognition, she really began to stop listening. She closed her ears to what he was saying. It was as if he were not speaking at all. He wasn't aware that she wasn't listening. He went on and on. At first she thought she couldn't stand it. She felt like hitting him over the head with something. If only he would shut up! But he wouldn't, and she couldn't bring herself to any physical action. She had tried to tell him what he was doing to her, but it was as if she hadn't spoken. So she began to close her ears to him. She retreated into her own silence. This went on for a year or two.

Gradually she began to discover that even when she wanted to hear what he was saying it was extremely difficult. Was she getting hard of hearing? She noticed that her friends all seemed to be shouting at her to make her hear and understand. It was true! She *was* getting hard of hearing.

What she did not know was that her body had simply followed the direction of her mind, and had begun to shut off her power to hear. It made no distinctions concerning what she was to hear. She had been living in an unchanging atmosphere in which it had been necessary to stop listening. The talent for not listening expressed itself in an inability to hear, and this became the general condition of her life.

She was thinking of getting a hearing-aid when her husband suddenly died of a heart attack. Now she was alone. The sounds around her were her own. Now there was no reason for shutting them out. An old French philosopher once observed, "I hate noise, unless I make it myself." She no longer hated noise. Almost immediately her hearing began to improve. Today she hears as well as anyone else. The primary cause of her inability to hear well had been eliminated instantly, and healing was hers.

### Alcoholism Can Also Be a Family-Factor Illness

Albert Sampson was slowly drinking himself to death. Out of a childhood history of rejection, neglect, and lack of love, he had acquired a sense of unworthiness and inadequacy. Through his destructive overindulgence, he was punishing himself for being alive. When he came to see me, it was as the last, desperate act of a man who was intelligent enough to know that deterioration and death were ahead of him unless something happened to help him overcome his habit.

My method was to change his attitude toward himself, and to get him to discard his false family-factor motive for self-punishment.

"Would you take an axe and beat the body of a friend's car to pieces?" I asked him.

"Of course not!" he answered.

"Would you put sugar in its gasoline tank?"

"I certainly would not," he said.

"Nevertheless," I told him, "you are beating your own body, and pouring into it that which is slowly ruining it. You think this body is yours, but it is only yours in trust. It is yours to use for a time, but in reality it belongs to God. It is the temple in which you enjoy life. You are doing to this body of God what you claim you would not do to the body of someone's car. Basically, however, the actions are the same. If you would not do these things to that organization of substances and materials called an automobile, why do them to the organization of substances and materials called your body? Neither one of them really belongs to you. If you are honorable in one sense, why not be honorable in the other? You may as well be consistent in your motives."

For Albert Sampson it was a new way of looking at what he was doing, and it helped him eliminate his destructive motives so that he could eliminate his destructive habit.

These represent only a minute fraction of the "family-factor" cases that have come to my attention. I have not even begun to give you the many sides of family involvements. As we have seen, some of them arise out of love, devotion, duty, responsibility; some out of irritation, hatred, fear, guilt, or unsatisfied need. Whatever the motive, whatever the primary cause behind them, their results can be deadly.

### Why the Home Is the Most Dangerous Place in the World

The home is not only the place where many of our ills have their origin. The National Safety Council reports that it also is the place where most of our accidents occur. Astronaut John Glenn orbited the earth without a scratch, yet he fell victim to a serious accident in his own home.

It is not suggested that we leave home to avoid accidents, any more than that we separate ourselves from our family in order to avoid illnesses. But we must remain aware that while the home is the most influential and beneficial of our institutions, it also is the most dangerous; some of our most destructive attitudes are acquired in it, and out of it are born some of our most destructive emotions.

### Twelve Suggestions for Avoiding or Healing Family-Factor Illnesses

1. Do not allow family emotions to reach the extremes of hysteria. (Hysterical optimism can be just as dangerous as hysterical pessimism.)

2. Do not allow family emotions to remain at or near one extreme level—either in a constant state of exhilaration, or in a constant state of depression. The resultant tension in a child (or an adult) can express itself in almost any illness.

3. Maintain a balanced concern for the welfare of your children. Do not smother them with care, or wilt them by neglect. Let them make some of their own decisions, and choose their own free, independent way of life.

4. Do not allow illness to give your children dominion over you or your family. At the same time, however, let no illness make your children feel guilty for having it.

5. Keep family conditions harmonious, so that the benefits of health far outweigh the benefits of illness. Participation in family work and responsibilities should be made to appear as an opportunity rather than as a task.

6. Give your children the benefit of training in sound, spiritual truths. Take them to some Sunday school; associate them and yourself with some church, and make your attendance regular.

7. Surround them with an atmosphere in harmony with spiritual truths. You cannot profess to believe in high ideals, yet practice their opposite, and expect your children to accept and follow your beliefs. Your life must be their example.

8. Make your life a reflection of your knowledge of such ideals and spiritual truths, so that it does not center itself

on illness-producing ideas, emotions, superstitions or beliefs.

9.  Recognize that while love of family is most commendable, and while love in general can be a great healing force, love wrapped in fear or nourished by possessiveness is unhealthy and destructive. Neither possess, nor be possessed. Do not allow your love to turn into fear of its loss. Do not acquire the smothering habit of over-protecting the person loved.

10. Realize that membership in a family does not mean an inescapable, unavoidable, or necessarily permanent association with it. You are first a child of God, and only secondarily a child of your parents. Your parents were God's agents for your creation, just as you are His agent for the creation of your own.

    There is "a time for every purpose," the preacher in Ecclesiastes tells us. There is a time to be a child, and a time to be an adult. "When I was a child," said Paul, "I spake as a child, I understood as a child, I thought as a child; but when I became a man, I put away childish things."

11. Live according to the laws and truths of life as given in this book, so that you have no room in your consciousness for any destructive feelings, attitudes, or ideas about anyone or anything, no matter how justified they may appear to be. The spiritual understanding that makes for spiritual certainty will not allow others to dominate, intimidate, stifle, possess, or sublimate you—either because of your love, need, fear, or hatred of them, or because of their love, need, fear, or hatred of you. Declare your mental, emotional, spiritual, and physical independence from all things, persons, places, times, beliefs, and conditions that can make you ill, and thus make you less than you truly are.

12. You do not ease the burden of pain in a loved one by consciously or subconsciously hurting yourself. No such compensation is great enough to justify it. The increase or multiplication of this world's suffering can never be justified on the basis of sympathy, guilt, or vengeance. Compassion for the illness or difficulty of another does not demand equal pain.

Certainly, it is difficult not to react emotionally when one member of your family is suffering in some way. You feel so close, so sympathetic, so sorry. But even in this reaction (the reaction of concern and love), you must be very careful. In the first place, you do not really help those who suffer by your suffering with them. Secondly, your belief in their suffering, and your acceptance of it, evident in your sympathy and sorrow, surrounds them with an even greater atmosphere of suffering, and makes them believe in it all the more. Furthermore, your emotion has an inevitably destructive effect upon yourself. It weakens you, makes you receptive to illness, attracts experiences to match or compensate for the illness of your loved ones. Your love and concern demands of you the best possible treatment you can give or acquire, and certainly a full measure of compassion. It leads you to seek the best means to relieve suffering and to heal its cause. But the one thing you cannot afford is to become so emotionally involved that you not only believe in the reality, danger, and staying-power of the problem, but that you compound its power by becoming a part of it yourself. Thousands of men and women are ill today because they did not have the spiritual understanding to separate themselves from a belief in the manifestation of the problem, and to join themselves with a belief in the power to heal it.

*Take action now* to heal the family-factor causes of illness by making (or marking) this set of healing ideas. They are your next step toward health and fulfillment.

## EVENING

*Tonight I surround myself and my home with harmony and love.*

*All irritating or restricting influences in my life have disappeared.*

*I am a free person in a world which is always a reflection of my own love, tolerance, and understanding.*

*I release every belief in the need or value of suffering, mine or that of anyone else.*

## MORNING

*I give thanks for this new day in which I am truly my own person.*

*I will not react destructively to anyone today.*

*There is peace, harmony, and freedom in every situation and in every member of my family.*

*Today I shall demonstrate my new maturity.*

*I shall not permit myself any destructive emotion, no matter how justified it may seem to be.*

## DAY

*This day I have "put away childish things."*

*I am neither* dependent *nor* independent.

> *But now I live an* inter-dependent *life—giving and receiving—helping and being helped—claiming my freedom and allowing others theirs.*

*I am not forced by any emotional pressures or needs to do that which is not right for me.*

*Today I discard every idea and belief that hurts me, even though it may come from those I love.*

*I no longer need to run away or to escape from problems. I meet and overcome them with my new sense of self-confidence and power.*

# 12

## How to Vanquish Protest
## and Guilt and Live a
## Longer, Happier Life

Were we to lose our freedom to protest some attitude or condition we think unfair, we would lose one of our most precious rights. Public protest is one of our major tools in checking discrimination of every kind. But when protest is suppressed, and at the same time charged with some negative emotion, anything can happen to lead to the destruction of the protestant.

### Rid Yourself of Both Just and Unjust Protest

It is the secret, unspoken, hidden protest that finds its means of expression in some subtle, dangerous way. A child may feel a sense of unfairness, that it is being unjustly or unduly disciplined, punished, or denied. Yet it has learned that to protest these things brings even more discipline, punishment and denial. It cannot publicly protest anything without running the risk of incurring parental disapproval and other painful results. So the protest is suppressed; but it does not go unexpressed. It breaks out in the only way over which the child

169

has any control—illness in its own body. It may develop hives, asthma, colds, stuttering, or some other illness or disease.

The adult who has not learned to make his protests unemotionally, and with the feeling that this is his right, regardless of the pressures that are put upon him to remain silent, may follow the same patterns as the child. His manifestations, however, may be of a more deadly kind—coronaries, paralysis, chronic asthma or hay-fever, blindness, kidney trouble, and so on. Although a coroner's report will list some other cause, death is often the result of some emotion-filled, yet silent, protest about something he feels he is publicly, officially, morally, financially, or socially powerless to change or resist. His greatest secret, destructive protest is against some "authority" which he cannot fight, and about which he feels a sense of frustration and futility.

A boy sets fire to his school. When caught and questioned, he readily admits that he did it "just for fun." Actually, however, it was his protest against the school, his teachers, or his parents.

A man hates his boss, but he is afraid of losing his job if he makes any kind of protest about what he thinks are unfair practices. Everything the boss does irritates him. He would like to go into his office some morning and "tell him off." But he suffers in silence. Eventually, his hatred and his irritation combine into one explosive protest: he has a heart-attack. Now he doesn't have to go back to work. He won the silent argument at the expense of his own security and health. And even he does not know why he had the attack.

## Take Command of Your Own Life

Mere public protest is not the answer. If there is to be protest, and it is not completely fulfilled and released within the secret thoughts of the protestant, it must be expressed in a creative, constructive way. It must carry some suggestions for correcting the condition protested, or it must make its point without the attachment of some destructive emotion. You may say, "How am I going to react pleasantly and constructively to someone I know is wrong—someone who seems bent on making me irritated and who does everything he can to get me upset?"

The answer is that no one has any power over you that you do not give him. It is not his action but your reaction that causes the irritation within you. You are the only one who can decide just how much influence the thoughts or actions of anyone else will have upon you. It cannot be repeated too often that *you* are the one who must take command of your own life, that you must never relinquish that command to anyone else for any reason. Do not give anyone or anything so much power that you lose control of yourself because of it. The loss of self-control, of self-possession, the loss of temper and a quiet, reasoning mind are the first losses on the way to the final loss of all your control over your own life.

Make no one so important to you that he dominates your emotions in some destructive way; that is, by making you irritated, angry, frustrated, fearful, disgusted, hurt, or discouraged.

Refuse to become emotionally disturbed by the commissions or omissions of those whom you have made important to you.

Do what you can to correct such commissions or omissions, but do so constructively, not with an antagonistic attitude. If correction of the condition does not seem feasible or possible, then begin to lessen the degree of its importance to *you*.

Remind yourself at these moments of protest that nothing has importance to you that you do not give it.

Realize that the destructive results lie within your own thoughts, not in some act or failure to act "out there."

### Be Spiritually Oriented
### in Dealing with Your Protest

When your protest is imbued with hate, your greatest freedom will come through forgiveness. This is the way of the
spiritually oriented, not the psychologically oriented. There are
schools of thought which tell us we should express our protest
and our hatred by aggressive actions against the images or
symbols of our hate. "Throw something at that picture of your
brother," a small boy is told. He is supposed to "get it out of
his system" that way. The question is: What put it into his
system in the first place? That is where the healing must begin.
Such release techniques are no more advanced than that of the
savage who sticks pins into an image of his enemy. This may
release the pent-up fury he feels, but it does not change the
cause of that fury; it does not release him of it permanently;
it does not lift or ennoble him. It is the primitive approach to
healing, and it has nothing but primitive results.

Nevertheless, such an approach is practiced constantly in
our own "civilized" society. Some men practice it when they
hang over a bar all night, getting themselves drunk, looking
for trouble, punishing themselves. Thus they mentally stick pins
into the lives of the wives whom they have learned to hate, or
with whom they have become merely bored.

Death-dealing protest lurks in the consciousness of a man
and wife who no longer love each other, but who stay together
for social, religious, or economic reasons. An insidious enmity
exists between them which works its slow poison into their
systems.

### The Long, Low-grade Protest Is Dangerous, Too

The secret, low-grade protest that endures for an extended
time may be just as dangerous as the suddenly explosive one.

Be wary of maintaining an attitude of constant protest about even the simpler things in life—where you live, how you look, the kind of work you are doing, the way a neighbor keeps his yard, the weather—any condition that may cause you to do a "slow burn." By such continued attitudes the very essence of life is burned out of your body. It may take years to manifest itself, but it is taking place, just the same.

### Roger Blakesley, and the Illnesses of His Protest

Roger Blakesley was an only child born into a family whose father was prominent professionally and whose mother was prominent socially. In the atmosphere of adult intensity, importance, and perfection in which he was raised, he began to feel inadequate and unworthy, as if he were in the way, unwanted, and a failure. The attention he received seemed directed only at his ineptness, childishness, and imperfections.

The things he liked to do, the things which interested him, were ridiculed because they were foreign to his father's profession, and were not flattering to his mother's position. He began to withdraw from contact with others, while at the same time throwing up signals for help and attention.

His withdrawal took the form of quietness, secretiveness, seclusion, and aloneness. If he could not be accepted for what he did, he would try not to be rejected simply by the process of doing nothing that others could observe and criticize. His signals for help and attention took the form of illness—asthmatic attacks, and arthritic pains.

He had a basically competitive nature. But his family-factor illnesses made it necessary for him to withdraw even from the games of his schoolmates. Because his withdrawal from the outer world was almost complete, and because his nature still wanted to express itself, for a while he created inner competitions to take the place of the outer ones he could not enter. He competed with himself by creating, and then opposing, his

desires. He competed with his environment by secretly pro-
testing everything it did and represented to him. Because his
desires had nowhere to go, and because his protests had no
real outlet or influence on anyone but himself, they broke out
in multiple pains and protracted wheezing. He became a
lonely, insignificant child in a busy, people-packed, significant,
demanding world.

His illnesses became substitutes for his sense of personal
growth and achievement. His father became austere, aloof, dis-
interested. His mother became domineering. They could not
give their son what he needed from them: credit for thinking
for himself.

His need to compete persisted, however. Without realizing
why he did it, he began to take long, solitary trips out into
the desert. He got as close to self-sufficient, isolated living as
he could. Here he not only nursed and satisfied his protest-
inspired desire to withdraw from life, but found the physical
competition he needed—storms, sun, hardships, privations.
Nature, completely unlike anything else he had ever known,
accepted him as an equal, as a worthy competitor. It conceded
nothing, but neither did it regard him contemptuously. The
weather challenged him without demanding his credentials.
The animals respected, feared, or were wary of him. To them
he was "The Great Hunter."

It wasn't surprising that the moment he left the city-limits
on one of these trips, he began to feel better. The spasms of
asthma eased and disappeared. The pains ceased. He was free.
He was "someone"—an individual, a man—not the "son," the
"little boy" of someone else. But the old pattern reappeared
when he returned to the city, and the illnesses persisted.

He grew up. He graduated from college. He became a
teacher. Teaching was not what his parents would have chosen
for him. He taught the very young, and found that they, at
least, regarded him with a measure of awe and respect. Even
now, however, he still needed the approval and respect of his

parents. Receiving at best only condescension, he continued to live under an emotional burden. His illnesses and pains recurred regularly.

One day he fell in love, and soon thereafter was married. Gradually, the realization of his physical, mental, and emotional freedom came to him. As he began to release his need for filial approval and to decrease his protest at not receiving it (in fact, his marriage itself was a declaration of his independence), the illnesses themselves began to decrease. They began to disappear because he had no more need for them. He had discovered a whole new world, and it was all his. He was receiving attention, adoration, respect, and love. He was Roger Blakesley, citizen, teacher, family-man, individual.

But then began a new series of troubles. At first they were intermittent, then almost regular virus attacks. Some new primary cause had developed.

He no longer took his long, solitary trips into the desert or the mountains. But what he did not realize was that his need for them had not ceased. His need for competition had, some-how, to express itself. It might be camouflaged, but it would not be submerged. Nowhere in life had he received any training for the usual modes of competition—sports, public speaking, plays—yet he had to find some channel for it. The trips done, nature no longer threatening, once again he found his competi-tion in about the only place left: within himself. Once again (in his virus attacks) he began to "compete" with himself against his desires, dreams, needs, ambitions, and responsi-bilities. The conflict swayed back and forth. He was well one week, ill the next. In a way, his attacks also were a protest against the marriage, a marriage which now denied him his right, his freedom to meet his old antagonist, nature.

### What Roger Blakesley Needed for His Healing

The solution for Roger Blakesley was not to be found in pills, potions, inhalants, exercises, or shots. It was to be found only within himself.

He needed to revise and reorganize his thinking, so that he could revise and reorganize his life.

He needed training in understanding himself, and a realization concerning the real primary causes within his own thoughts.

He needed a spiritual insight into his own nature as a free, self-determining, unlimited child of God.

He needed the incentive to find some constructive channel for his competitive urges, and the courage to follow it.

He needed the willingness to release old habit patterns by facing them, and claiming his superiority over them.

To sum up all this: he needed to know (and to practice) the principles upon which this book is written.

It was my privilege to begin working with Roger Blakesley at this stage of his life. The old beliefs and habit patterns were stubborn. The old ideas were difficult to release. The old protests were deeply ingrained. The basic needs were long suppressed, and their satisfaction warped. But after his conscientious effort to understand the primary causes of his illnesses, he began to realize *why* he had been ill so long.

He is now studying and practicing the ideas that you are studying and practicing through this book. When he has absorbed them to the point where they become part of him— where they seem completely natural and right to him—he will reach that sudden, exhilarating moment in which he will say, with an instantaneous recognition, "I am healed!"

### Expel Your Guilt—Founded and Unfounded

Alice Naughton, the sickly child among her brother and two sisters, was never really well at any time during her first forty-nine years of life. She lived also with the feeling that she was unwanted, unnecessary, and rejected. She suffered a deep sense of guilt for having been born.

Nearing her fiftieth birthday, she became so ill that everyone, including herself, thought she would die. In moments of consciousness between the medicine and the pain, she did some thinking she had never dared to do before, and she had some questions that never before had occurred to her. She called her mother to her bedside and put the questions to her. Why, she asked, had she been treated so badly all her life? Why had she been made to feel so worthless and unwanted? Why was her family always so callous, so cruel? What had she done? Had she made some sort of mistake simply by being alive?

The answer seemed unbelievable, yet she had to believe it because there was no other answer that seemed possible to explain the treatment she had received from her father and mother.

Because her daughter was going to die anyway, the mother decided to disclose a long-held secret. "You were born on Christmas Day," her mother told Alice coldly, "Christ's birthday. Your father and I felt it was some kind of sign that you should suffer as Christ suffered."

It was a fantastically fanatic reason. Yet, for them it had been good enough. Forty-nine years of imposed suffering because of the coincidence of a Christmas birth!

But it was not good enough for Alice Naughton. She was weak in body and low in spirit, but her eyes were opened. She should have had a happy life, not a sad one. She should have lived in the reflection of the glory of Christ, not under the shadow of his suffering. There was no reason for her sense of guilt. There was every reason to feel wanted and confident in the light of her joyous birth. God wanted her! she exclaimed to herself. What did it matter now that her parents had believed as they had?

From that moment on, Alice Naughton began to get well. Because she had recognized her sense of guilt for the false thing it was, and because she declared her freedom from mental, emotional and spiritual domination, her physical being also was free, and she became a well, mature, and happy woman.

The guilt-ridden person is one whose health is in deadly danger. It makes no difference whether his sense of guilt is justified or not. There are men and women like Alice Naughton, literally dying of guilt, who have committed no serious errors at all. Self-condemnation becomes self-punishment, and through the inevitable justice of the subconscious mind, the healthy cells of the body begin to be sick; they go perverse, get out of balance, lose their strength, wither, or die.

Good analysts, counsellors, and practitioners are constantly alert for the guilt-factor in a client's unwanted experiences or sick states of mind. The feeling of guilt, however, is one of the most difficult to uncover because men and women try to keep their guilts hidden to the last. They do not want to reveal to anyone their dark thoughts about what they have done or failed to do.

### How Guilt Can Be Used as a Tool or a Weapon

There is nothing wrong or neurotic about feeling guilty, provided such a guilt feeling is not unreasonable, extreme, or prolonged. There is, however, something insidious in feeling guilty for feeling guilty.

There are times when we yield to unreasonable demands, bow to psychological dictators, or succumb to emotional blackmail in order not to feel guilty. The dominant emotion then becomes fear of guilt, which is as destructive as guilt itself. A degree of guilt, or at least an ability to feel guilty, is necessary to all of us if civilization is to survive. The absence of some guilt, or a weak capacity for guilt shows a dangerous lack of a sense of responsibility, and without our sense of responsibility all the values we hold dear are doomed.

The capacity for guilt can save us from the chaos of irresponsibility, yet, the practice of guilt can lead us to the chaos of torture, suffering, and self-punishment. We must understand the tool of guilt, so that it does not become the weapon.

### Realize Guilt Comes in Strange Guises

Every person creates his own causes or reasons for feeling guilty. They may be completely different from those of anyone else. For him, however, they are important to his way of life and his peace of mind. Others may laugh at the things about which he feels guilty, but for him they are the values upon which he rests his existence.

For example, Clete Daniels invested $10,000 in a partnership, against the judgment and desires of his wife. The partnership failed. He lost the $10,000. Thereafter, he was engulfed in guilt, not because of the $10,000 he lost, but because he didn't listen to his wife. She helped him remember his mistake.

Mary Sheffield decided to reduce. She selected a certain highly-recommended diet. Soon after she began following the diet, she was offered her favorite dessert. She ate it, but felt so guilty about eating it that she didn't enjoy it.

Mary's friend also decided to reduce. She chose her favorite diet. But she was unable to resist food. She sneaked into the kitchen at night so that she could eat under the cover of darkness. She couldn't face her feelings of guilt in the daylight.

A talented soprano felt so guilty for having married, thus ruining an opportunity to become a great opera singer (which was the dream of her mother), that she punished herself by making her marriage fail.

The president of a large corporation allowed a completely unfair situation to cause the resignation under fire of one of the senior executives. He withheld the facts which would have cleared the other man because he was afraid of the man's threat to his own position in the company. But his sense of guilt became stronger each week. Driving home one day he caused an "accident" in which he broke his back. He was never able to return to the office again.

Destructive consequences of a feeling of guilt—founded or unfounded, justified or unjustified—may be found in failure, unhappiness, frustration, disappointment, accidents, illness, and death.

### Suggestions for the Guilt-Ridden

If you feel guilty for any reason, you are in danger. No one may ever discover your real or assumed guilt, but *you* know it.

If, therefore, you feel guilty, as Paul said, "Think on these things. . . ."

There is only today. Guilt is a form of hanging on to the past, perpetuating a destructive memory, spoiling the reality of today with the unreality and the errors of yesterday.

Guilt is worship of the God of "gone." Forgiveness (given and accepted) is love of the spirit of "here."

It is as blessed to accept forgiveness as it is to forgive. One is incomplete without the other. Many persons are suffering today for some wrong they did to another, even though the other long ago forgave. The acceptance of forgiveness is really all that is necessary to one who feels guilty, for true forgiveness comes not from man or woman, but from God. "Father, forgive them, for they know not what they do," said Jesus. He did not say, "I forgive them," but "Father, forgive them."

Is there, in your consciousness, the memory of some wrong, some error, slight, omission, or commission which has left its residue of guilt? Whatever it was, accept your forgiveness now. Accept it not just from man or woman, but from God.

If there is anything you are doing today about which you feel guilty, then stop doing it, or analyze your guilt to see whether it is reasonable and just. If your analyzation leads you to conclude that your guilt is unfounded and unjust, or that it is out of date and unjust, release yourself from its grip.

*"I have finished with this guilt, and it has finished with me,"* you may say. *"I am free of the past because the person I was in that past is not the person I am today. I refuse to suffer for what I am not, and something I would not do today. I am forever free of the false claims of this guilt. I release it, reject it, and let it go. It is no more a part of my consciousness."*

It may be that you will find that your sense of guilt is well-founded, reasonable, up to date, and just. Then first seek forgiveness from within and, as Jesus advised, "Go and sin no more." (John 8:11.) You may hide what you are doing from the world, but you cannot hide it from your own conscience and consciousness. Get in harmony with these, and you will be in harmony with your world. Resolve your conflicts by choosing between them, and by being worthy of your choice.

Finally, *don't live today what you regret of yesterday. Rather, make today what you will want to remember tomorrow.*

To help make all your tomorrows memorable, use these healing ideas.

## EVENING

*I have deserted forever my former deadly companions—protest and guilt.*

*Tonight I am not against anything, but I am for everything that will make the negative and destructive conditions of life unnecessary or impossible.*

*Tonight I forgive everyone who has ever done anything wrong. Tonight I forgive myself for all my past errors and wrongs, against others or against myself. I am free of all my past burdens of guilt, because from this moment on I "go, and sin no more."*

## MORNING

*This is my day of forgiveness. I will not live today what I regret of yesterday, but I will make today what I shall want to remember tomorrow.*

*Whatever yesterday's faults or failings may have been, this is a new day in which my body and my mind are free to do the best they can.*

## DAY

*Today I direct all my energies not in protest, but in help; not in criticism, but in efforts to change what is destructive for what is constructive.*

*All past guilts are gone because of my acceptance of forgiveness given and received. I do not change yesterday by feeling guilty about it. Therefore I am now completely free of the guilt that has no connection with my life today. I do not live today what I regret of yesterday.*

# 13

## How You Can Prevent and Heal Some Prevalent Illnesses

### The Common Cold

The cold is so common because it can be instigated by almost any negative emotion. Big businesses, with their large offices crammed with employees, are warehouses for colds or the flu, because the pressures, irritations, fears, and jealousies of such groups are daily companions of the job. Often it takes only a small emotion to furnish the primary cause for the onslaught of a cold or an attack of the flu. All the ordinarily blamed causes—cold feet, drafts, wet weather, etc.—are only secondary causes, ". . . else," as John Caius said in 1552, "if one were sick, all should be sick."

*Worry* about anything, extended over even so much as a 24-hour period, can make the body subject to a cold.

*Sudden shocks,* or *unexpected emotional challenges* can do the same thing.

*Tension* of any kind that is not used constructively can break down the body's resistance to colds.

Most bodies have some point or points of weakness through which they are susceptible to certain illnesses and diseases. This

183

is why some persons run the cycles of heart trouble, others of kidney diseases, others of stomach disorders, still others of circulation problems, and so on.

The defense against the "common cold" is one of the body's most vulnerable points, and usually is the first to collapse when some emotional problem attacks it.

The person who wants to avoid the regular seasonal sessions of the flu, or the recurrent periods of a runny nose, must be one whose emotions are not just tightly controlled, suppressed, or held in check (for this is destructive also), but one who does not allow himself to be disturbed or upset by every little thing that happens or fails to happen. He is in complete command of himself, and he is not moved to some negative emotion as a result of what happens to or around him.

The person who is not subject to colds is one who is greater than his environment, who does not enter emotionally into all the office intrigue, gossip, politics, jealousy, bitterness, or criticism, and who refuses to get upset by anything.

This is not an easy state of mind to reach, but it can be reached with the consistent practice of these principles. Everything in this book is intended to lead you to this healing and healthful state of mind.

## Healing Attitudes and Beliefs for the Common Cold:

"My body and my life are free from all disturbing influences.

"This cold that has attached itself to me does not belong to me. I refuse to claim it by saying, 'My cold.' I reject it now, as I reject any and all negative ideas or emotions that may have attracted it to me.

"Everyone around me may have a cold, but I do not accept this as a sign that I, too, must have one. I do not accept the 'average' or the 'normal' for me.

"This cold is a reflection of some destructive emotion in me. I therefore speak this word for my peace of mind, knowing that nothing has the power to irritate me.

"I refuse to be caught up in, and to become a part of the confusion that may surround me.

"Because I know that Divine Wisdom is my inspiration, and that Divine Guidance is always with me, I do not worry about anything. I may be concerned; I may be careful; I may do what seems to be necessary or advisable to avoid or to correct some unwanted situation or condition, but I will not worry about it. I realize that when I worry about something, I merely surround *it* with my negative prayers, and make *myself* receptive to illness.

"I am at peace with my world."

### Arthritis

Perhaps the simplest way to describe a common form of arithritis is by saying that it is the result of the collection of calcium deposits at the wrong places in the body. The calcium that is beneficial when it is distributed correctly throughout the bones and the body, becomes dangerous and pain-inflicting when it collects incorrectly on the bones or at the joints. This of course refers only to the secondary (physical) cause.

There are several possible primary (mental and emotional) causes. Each person threatened with arthritis, or already suffering from it, may analyze his own emotions, beliefs, and thought-patterns to discover the primary cause of his illness. More than likely he will find one or more of the following primary causes:

1. *Rigidity:* inability to compromise, even with himself; stubbornness; pride.
2. *Stubbornness:* refusal to change actions, habits, or opinions, even when proved wrong. For example, the parent who stiffens in his attitude toward his children's search for their own way of life; the person who hardens his mind against someone or some thing.

   The arthritic is often one who makes up his mind and sticks with it. He rarely admits there are two sides to anything.

A report in *Newsweek* (April 27, 1959) gave this account of Christian A. Herter, then newly-appointed 60th U.S. Secretary of State: "Outwardly he's a gentle man, softspoken, almost shy, this tall, gray-haired New Englander, crippled by arthritis . . . but there's a core of cold steel behind (his) Boston Brahmin manner. And if Soviet Premier Khrushchev or Communist China's Mao Tse-tung think he's a man they can push around, they will have cause to regret their optimism."

3. *Fear:* stiffening of the backbone in times of danger or crisis. Some persons make everything a crisis, and constantly are clenching their fists, bracing themselves, getting ready for expected battle.

4. *Domination, dictatorialism:* assuming the attitude of the indomitable, inflexible will over others; unbending attitudes toward anything.

5. *The sanctity of established routine:* the hard and fast attitude toward the status quo; no ability to change pace.

6. *Wrong placement:* (see discussion of this belief on page 143.) The calcium deposits that cause a common form of arthritis are made of *good material* in the *wrong place*.

7. *Obstruction and delay:* (see discussion of this belief on page 141.) The calcium that normally flows through the body by means of the blood stream is obstructed and delayed in wrong places, particularly at the joints.

8. *Rigid restrictions, bondage, "imprisonment":* A letter to the editor of one of our large metropolitan newspapers said this: "For several years I had arthritis, which recently cleared up. Looking back, I realized that the arthritis disappeared at the same time I paid off the mortgage on my home. The period of the arthritis was the same length as the period of the mortgage."

Any feeling of being hemmed in, trapped, or of being caught in a situation where it seems impossible to extricate yourself places you in danger of developing arthritis. Any rigidity in mind, regardless of the reason, begins to reflect itself in rigidity in the body.

Arthritis is sometimes called hereditary. It appears so because members of the same family grow up under the same influences, atmosphere, and emotional environment, and are therefore mainly susceptible to the same tendencies, emotions, and illnesses.

*Healing Attitudes and Beliefs for Arthritis:*

"Everyone has a right to live the way he wants to live, and so do I.

"I recognize that everything changes; therefore, I do not stubbornly hold to any idea. I am always open to new truths, new ways, new ideas.

"I do not dominate anyone, nor do I allow myself to be dominated.

"I will not become a fanatic.

"I do not protect my pride at the expense of either experience or mental, emotional, and spiritual growth.

"I am flexible in my attitudes. I am always in my right place.

"Life and its good flows through my life happily, easily, effortlessly, and abundantly now."

### Other Health-Ruining Effects and Their Probable Primary Causes

The preceding examples of human illnesses and their primary causes should be enough to give you an insight into the mysterious relationship between your thoughts and the changing conditions of your body. If you want an INSTANTANEOUS HEALING you must be sure that you do not continue the negative and destructive thoughts, ideas, attitudes, and emotions that made you receptive to illness in the first place.

Keeping your thoughts clear, fresh, and uncontaminated is more than just a moral issue. Upon this depends the health and safety of life. To repeat the theme of this book: "Think as if your life depends upon it, because it does!"

In the first part of this chapter you were given a list of primary causes and some of their potential results. To close this chapter, I would like to give you a brief list of some specific results (illnesses and diseases) and their probable primary causes. If the illnesses noted are those for which you need healing, check the probable primary causes carefully. Then review the habit patterns and tendencies of your own thoughts, ideas, attitudes, and emotions. If you find those which apply to you, begin immediately to eliminate them. Do this by consciously changing the level and direction of your thoughts, bearing in mind the suggestions given throughout this book. Once again, let me remind you that it will do no permanent good to dose or cut out an effect, if the primary cause is not removed as well. *Operate on your thoughts, and it may not be necessary to operate on your body.*

| EFFECTS | PROBABLE PRIMARY CAUSE OR CAUSES |
|---|---|
| Heart attacks | *Emotional Stress,* brought on by: |
| Hypertension | Ambition, |
| Heart palpitations | The struggle for success, |
| | Fear of failure, |
| | Deadline pressures, |
| | Demands for "busyness," |
| | Desire to escape some |
| |    duty, |
| |    responsibility, or |
| |    unpleasant situation. |
| |    ( Good starter—poor finisher) |
| | Worry, |
| | Anger, temper |
| | Hatred, |

|  | Impatience, |
|  | Jealousy, |
|  | A sense of overload, |
|  | Sensitivity (feelings easily hurt), |
|  | Persistent unhappiness, |
|  | Belief in obstruction and delay. |
| Allergies | Feelings of restriction, |
| Skin rashes | Unresolved resentment and |
| Hives | hostility, |
| Eczema | A sense of inadequacy and |
|  | inferiority, |
|  | Belief in being pushed into or |
|  | trapped in an unwanted |
|  | situation, |
|  | Irritation, |
|  | Frustrating emotional situations, |
|  | Grudge-carrying, |
|  | Resistance to authority. |
| Ulcers | Job or family stress, |
|  | Financial stringency, |
|  | Fear of not doing a good job, |
|  | Irritation, |
|  | Temper, |
|  | Overload. |
| Diabetes | Belief in wrong action, |
|  | Sense of imbalance in affairs, |
|  | Frustration, |
|  | Lack of conviction and faith, |
|  | Easily discouraged. |
| Tiredness, depletion | Futility, |
|  | "Give-up-itis," |
|  | Overload. |

Here are your healing ideas for use in eliminating destructive primary causes in your life.

●–●–●–●–●–●–●–●–●–●–●–●–●–●–●–●–●–●–●–●–●–●–●–●–●–●–●–●–●–●–●–●–●–●–●–

## EVENING

*I now declare that I am free of all the disturbing influences of this day. I am calm and at peace.*

*In the quiet of this night, all things move in the right way to their rightful places. I sleep in the midst of an ordered, harmonious universe.*

●–●–●–●–●–●–●–●–●–●–●–●–●–●–●–●–●–●–●–●–●–●–●–●–●–●–●–●–●–●–●–●–●–●–

## MORNING

*This coming day will hold only pleasant experiences for me. My emotions are all constructive. Today I will not react destructively to anything.*

*Everything is in its right place. As I move through places, as I pass men and women, as I meet problems, I know that everything will express only love, harmony and helpfulness. I welcome this day with expectation and faith.*

●–●–●–●–●–●–●–●–●–●–●–●–●–●–●–●–●–●–●–●–●–●–●–●–●–●–●–●–●–●–●–●–●–●–

## DAY

*I am completely immune—physically, mentally, and emotionally—to all the negative ideas, beliefs or experiences that may be around me. They have no part of me.*

*This day I give freedom to the world, as I claim it for myself.*

*I am flexible in all things. This is a world of change, and I am always willing to change myself and my ideas for a better self and a better world.*

●–●–●–●–●–●–●–●–●–●–●–●–●–●–●–●–●–●–●–●–●–●–●–●–●–●–●–●–●–●–●–●–●–●–

### Are You Ready?

Have you been courageous enough to follow the suggestions for self-discovery given in this chapter? Are you willing to recognize the causes for your illness, and eliminate them? Then *you are ready to exercise your inborn authority.*

# 14

## Achieving Instantaneous Healing Through Thinking and Speaking with Authority

You were born with the authority to think and speak for yourself. Are you using it?

When you speak with authority, when you say, "I am well; I have overcome all the bad attitudes, ideas, fears, and beliefs that brought this illness to me in the first place," you are *practicing* your authority. But if you have reservations, if you allow yourself to doubt the result, you are not actually *using* it.

### How the Healing Power Responds to Your Authority

When you make a faith-filled demand upon the eternal powers that surround and flow through you, something inevitable begins to happen on the hidden side of life. The power to heal instantly responds to the authority with which you claim and direct it.

But that power requires your strength. It will not respond, except in a negative way, to your weakness. Do not be afraid that you are not strong enough. Do not protest that you are weak. Be modest about yourself as a personality if you wish, but do not put any limitations upon the inner person you really are. Life does not judge you and withhold its blessings except as you judge yourself and withhold those blessings from yourself.

Jesus spoke "as one having authority," because he thought with authority. It was through the authority of his thought that the "miracles" were achieved.

You have the same authority that Jesus had. If you will read his words again carefully you will see that even He told you this. You may call upon the creative, healing power within you ("the Father within") just as He did.

### Doubt Weakens Your Authority

If you have allowed yourself the slightest doubt about your right to that healing power, or your authority to call upon and expect the perfect healing of your illness or disease, you have denied and rejected an authority that is above every court, every legal document, every man-made law, regulation, restriction, or limitation that is now or ever has been in existence.

The conquest of your illness is nothing but the peaceful conquest of yourself. You must, through the principles of this book, overcome the destructive tendencies you have acquired and nurtured. Stop fighting yourself. Stop denying yourself. Give up your claims of inadequacy, inferiority, weakness. "Every Kingdom divided against itself is brought to desolation; and a house divided against itself falleth."

### Hope Is Not Enough

When you say, "I am well," do not divide yourself against yourself even by following it with "I hope." Hope is a beautiful word, but it always contains a measure of doubt. For your instantaneous healing you can entertain no doubts.

Forget the little *I* that has failed and grown ill before. There is a new premise in your life; a new you that you have only now discovered. That new you is the real you, the one with unlimited authority to claim the happiness, prosperity and health it wants.

Do you need a miracle in your life—the healing of an illness ... the meeting of a financial crisis ... the return of something lost ... the discovery of love ... the release of some serious emotional problem ... the conquering of a habit? Whatever it is—large or small, major or minor—the miracle can happen for you here and now, even though the evidence is yet to be seen. Forget yourself for a moment. Stop remembering your fears, failures, doubts, and limitations. Get out of the past. Submerge yourself completely in a consciousness of the unlimited power that created you and that has never deserted you.

### Use Your Imagination

Imagine for a moment that you as a separate personality with a history, memory, and experiences have ceased to exist. Now you are an inseparable, indivisible part of infinite, unlimited, all-embracing power. In you there is no human weakness. You are united with that in which there is no illness, failure, crisis, sorrow, or fear. It is the time of the miracle; for the miracle comes when, through an intensity of inspiration you shed your individual human self, and you forget that you were once someone who couldn't, who suffered, or who was afraid. You become a part of the perfect, unlimited Infinite, in which the "miracle" is only the reflection of an unlimited belief. I challenge you to try it!

If you need words to express these feelings and these thoughts, I suggest something like the following:

*From this instant, I no longer am the person who was ill, lonely, confused, hurt, or habit-bound. The limited consciousness, the restricted faith, the sense-pained body, the mental anguish, the emotional and physical suffering that belonged to that person who was called myself a moment ago no longer are true of the self I am right now. I have lost that old fearful, problem-ridden, discouraged identity, I have become whole, perfect, free. I choose this miracle with complete confidence, because I have confidence in that which has the power to make it a commonplace. I do not judge myself by my past, but by what I am and what I can be. I do not choose hesitantly, but through the divine authority with which, by the grace of God, I have been invested. I choose what I want, then surrender myself to the miraculous power to achieve it within me. Nothing—not even my old self, my past consciousness, my former mistakes or yesterday's failures—can keep it from me. I choose, believe, claim, accept, receive, and give thanks for it now.*

(Mark this place with a slip of paper, and return to it often.)

### Demonstrate Your Strength

Never permit yourself to become so wrapped up in your misery that you forget your authority to overcome it. Do not let your mind become so filled with the awareness of your weakness or suffering that you have little capacity left for the awareness of your healing power.

If you want even more assurance, you need only look around you at what is happening in this world today. We have more reason to believe in our unlimited potential than at any other time in our history. Physical barriers are falling; records are being broken every day; intellectual limitations are receding; we are constantly forming new concepts of our intellectual powers. Even spiritual boundaries disappear when we take dominion over the forces of evil in our own thinking. There will be still more records, overrun barriers, new intellectual horizons, mental concepts, and spiritual dimensions, when we recognize and use the Infinite Power that is resident in every mind, released in every thought, and expressed in every experience. That our experiences have been less than what we would like them to be, that the miracles have been missing, can be attributed to our failure to improve our concepts of what life really is, and recognize our authority to use the power life gives us.

Today, then, you can discard the weakness of unworthy thinking, and demonstrate your strength to life. You can "call the bluff" of that which seems to say: "You can't," and "I'll destroy you if you try."

### Choose Your Own Miracle

Have you said, "Nothing but a miracle will help me?" Then choose it! Do not be afraid it cannot be done. Do not judge Infinite Power by the weakness of yesterday's human faith. When you stop limiting the Infinite you will stop limiting yourself.

Your INSTANTANEOUS HEALING is waiting for you.

Claim it.

Believe in it.

Accept it.

Clear your thoughts of all imperfect, unreal, or ill ideas and beliefs.

Now you have contacted the deeper things. You have gone beyond the sensory world, beyond past fictions and fallacies, into the reality of life. Here is true health. Here is perfection, beyond the limits of ignorance and superstition.

But do not omit or forget that you, too, must declare your triumph over your problems "as one having authority." If you forget it, all the complicated structures of study and knowledge will collapse in the face of illness. But if you remember and apply it, you will have made use of one of the great secrets so often overlooked by those who dream of healing and desperately hope for it, but who forever remain locked in the stubborn grip of illness and disease.

Use this secret of healing by thinking and speaking with *authority*.

To improve your sense of authority, use the following healing ideas tonight, tomorrow morning, and during the day.

•-•-•-•-•-•-•-•-•-•-•-•-•-•-•-•-•-•-•-•-•-•-•-•-•-•-•-•-•-•-•-•-•-•

## EVENING

*I know the perfect healing is waiting for me. Tonight, I speak these words with an inborn, God-given authority: "I am whole. I am well. I am free."*

•-•-•-•-•-•-•-•-•-•-•-•-•-•-•-•-•-•-•-•-•-•-•-•-•-•-•-•-•-•-•-•-•-•

## MORNING

*Today I shall so live that I am worthy of the healing authority I possess. I shall think and do nothing that is in conflict with the perfect pattern of health that I want.*

•-•-•-•-•-•-•-•-•-•-•-•-•-•-•-•-•-•-•-•-•-•-•-•-•-•-•-•-•-•-•-•-•-•

## DAY

*Every moment of this day is a witness to my Divine authority to live it in health, in happiness, and in peace.*

*I claim my healing. I accept it. I believe in it for me. I make myself worthy to receive it.*

•-•-•-•-•-•-•-•-•-•-•-•-•-•-•-•-•-•-•-•-•-•-•-•-•-•-•-•-•-•-•-•-•-•

# 15

## Using the Thankful Attitude to Gain Long-Lasting Health Protection

Two men who lived in the same apartment building awoke at the same hour one spring morning. One man looked out the window at the brilliant sunshine. "Good morning, God!" he said. The other looked out at the glaring light. "Good God! Morning!" he exclaimed.

There we have the difference between those who get well, and those who remain ill. The first man looked to his day with anticipation and expectation. Already he had the thankful attitude of one who knows his day will be filled with happiness and satisfaction. The other looked forward with repulsion and disgust. Nothing but boredom, irritation, and odious duty awaited him. He expected only the negative, unwanted experiences. There was not one bit of thankfulness in his whole attitude, because he didn't expect anything worth being thankful for.

Begin right now to practice the thankful attitude. Don't wait for life to prove to you that you have something for which to be thankful. Life will never get past such a demonstration of your pessimism and doubt.

### Use the Thankfulness, Not the "Wait-and-See," Method

In addition to the connection between thankfulness and enthusiasm, there is a connection between thankfulness and treatment. Effective prayer (treatment) for healing is not a supplication, entreaty, or petition; it does not require pleading or begging. It is based upon faith about that which you may not see. Otherwise, it is merely a ritual in which hope and doubt often play the biggest parts. Many pray or treat "on the chance that it might work," or "just in case there might be something to it." They don't want to miss any bets. They are the ones who reserve their thankfulness with a "wait-and-see" attitude. Such "spiritual insurance," underwritten by a shaky consciousness, seldom matures, and rarely pays off.

The man who treats for healing, and then withholds his thankfulness until he sees whether he really gets well, blocks that healing by his doubts and uncertainties, and by his unwillingness to accept the authority and power of his own mind. Such a man may go to his office and dictate a letter to someone known to him only by name, in some distant city. "Thanking you in advance . . ." he will say. He has more faith in a stranger, 3,000 miles away, than he has in the healing power within himself.

"I'd be so thankful," a woman will say, "if I could just get well." The probability of her healing would be increased a thousand-fold were she to say, "I am thankful *now* for the healing I *know* is mine." The highest demonstration of faith is thankfulness for that which we do not yet see, and have not yet experienced. "Faith is the substance of things hoped for," wrote Paul in his letters to the Hebrews, "the evidence of things not seen."

An error of thanksgiving is found in reserving it exclusively for that which has already occurred. It is an error because, used this way, it is concerned only with what has happened in the past, or that our senses tell us we possess now. Anyone can be thankful for what he has received, for what he can see or presently experience. It takes faith to be thankful for what we cannot see, and do not yet experience. This is the kind of faith, however, that creates miracles. Thankfulness is always a part of effective prayer, for, if nothing else, it is an evidence of faith.

### Place Your Order for Healing Now

You have already discovered that your credit for health is always good. Do not neglect to use that credit. If you have established an account at a large department store, there may come a day on which you will wish to use your credit there. Suppose that you have seen a newspaper advertisement by that department store describing a certain bedspread you would like to have. You pick up the telephone, call the order desk at the store, and request that the spread be delivered. When the order-clerk acknowledges you and tells you that it will be delivered as you requested, more than likely you end the transaction by saying, "Thank you." When you hang up the telephone, you have a sense of ownership. There is the distinct and unquestioned feeling that the bedspread is yours. Of course, you have not seen it. You do not have it in your hands. You cannot touch or in any way experience it physically. Yet, you have the positive, unshakable feeling that it is yours. When you say "Thank you," you make an affirmation of this feeling.

The same sense of ownership must accompany your "order" for healing and health. Even though the physical facts tell you that you are still sick, you must complete your order—your treatment—with the same conviction of possession and accomplishment that you did when you hung up the telephone. You may not see or experience the whole, complete body you want, any more than you could see or touch the bedspread. Nevertheless, your natural reaction, if you believe in the reality of either the expected bedspread or your expected healing, will be to say, "Thank you." *Practice saying this "Thank you" with your treatment for healing.* It will help you reach that point where you can accept, without question, that inevitable instant of healing you desire.

### How to Live Your Thankfulness

The truly thankful person lives a completely thankful life. He is not constantly talking to himself about how thankful he is, nor dedicating only certain days, hours, or situations to his thankfulness. He is quietly and steadily thankful within. It is a state of being, in which he accepts his good, expects his good, and respects his good.

Thanksgiving is a neglected talent. So many take for granted the blessings they have, because they are lost in their scramble for more. You may remember the story of the two angels who came to earth looking for prayers. One carried a basket in which he was to gather prayers of petition, supplication, and begging. The other came looking for prayers of thanksgiving. When they returned to heaven, the first angel's basket was filled to overflowing. The second angel's basket was almost empty.

Some will ask, "What have I got to be thankful for?" Each one of us can make his own list of personal blessings, whether he knows it or not. Opportunities, challenges, life itself, hold numberless blessings. When one opportunity fades, another will appear. Every life has its needs. Our needs show that we are alive. With our needs we face challenges. Needs and challenges often lead to prayer (treatment) while satisfaction of these needs, and the successful meeting of the challenges they create, often lead to thankfulness.

You want the prayers concerned with your needs and challenges answered. Why not assure their answer, their success, by your faith? "Thy faith hath made thee whole." How do you demonstrate your faith? By your thankfulness, not only *after* the fact, but *before.*

Once again, the INSTANTANEOUS HEALING you want is waiting for your order. Your next thought will connect you with an Infinite supply.

Claim your healing.

Believe in it for you.

Accept it.

You may not actually feel one bit better at this moment, but the fulfillment of your order is on its way.

Give thanks for it *now!*

This is all that remains for you to discover and to apply this secret of INSTANTANEOUS HEALING today.

Here is your final set of healing ideas. When you have completed them all, use them singly or in groups. But always keep them readily available. Because they will be the means of helping you conquer every illness, and then of allowing you to live a truly healthy life, they will be among your most precious possessions.

---

## EVENING

*I give thanks for everything good this day has brought me.*

*I give thanks for this night in which I can renew my strength for a wonderful day tomorrow.*

*I give thanks for the healing that is taking place in me now. Thank you!*

---

## MORNING

*I give thanks for this new day, and that I am privileged to live it.*

*Today I shall practice the* thankful attitude. *I shall look for anything and everything for which I can be thankful.*

*The smallest thing will not be too small to escape my thanks.*
*Thank you!*

<hr>

## DAY

*I give thanks for every unknown good which this day is*
*   bringing me.*
*I have a sense of ownership of all things I desire. They are*
*   mine, even though I do not see them and cannot experi-*
*   ence them at this moment.*
*I live a thankful life.*
*Thank you!*

<hr>

# 16

## Put Your Illness-Prevention
## Kit to Work Every Day

"All I can say, Mrs. Jones, is that it was just a wrong diagnosis. What we thought was some serious trouble turned out to be nothing at all. I'm sorry we had you so concerned, but I'm happy to report that there is absolutely nothing wrong with you."

Mrs. Jones is typical of many men and women who have received threatening notices of illness and come to me asking for help. After some treatment, and occasionally a period of intensive study with me, they have returned to their doctors for more tests, only to be told that the original diagnosis was in error.

Thereafter, some of them are like the man who was working on a steep, high roof. He started to slide toward the edge, and a long and dangerous drop to some rocks below. Quickly he prayed. "Oh, God, don't let me fall off this roof and I'll promise anything you want! Please, please stop me!" A moment later, as he was about to plunge over the edge, his belt caught on a nail, and he was saved. "Never mind, God," he said, "I got caught on a nail!"

If, when you finish this book, you find that some old illness that has been bothering you is gone, you may say, "I would have gotten over it anyway." Very well. The important thing is that you got well. Let the credit fall where it may. As Omar said, "Take the cash, and let the credit go."

### Check Your Life-Attitude

Mrs. John McEllen had a morbid fascination with the passing of her friends. She always turned first to the obituary column of the local newspaper. Once she went to a neighboring state to visit her daughter's family. But she was miserable her whole time there. Restless, lonesome, and obviously unhappy, she cut her visit short by a week. When she stepped off the train after arriving home, her husband was on the platform to meet her. Without acknowledging his greeting, or offering one of her own, she had only one question: "Anybody die?"

Mrs. McEllen never really enjoyed life. She was too wrapped up in the prospect of death. After all, she argued, for her this life was nothing but a long struggle, a vale of tears, and merely the prelude to heaven and her reward. Reward? For what?

Mrs. McEllen's attitude toward life was an attitude of death. Others have the "sick" attitude, the "failure" attitude, the "heartbreak" attitude, the "rejected," the "neglected," or the "victimized" attitude. Each one spoils the life that could be happy, prosperous, and healthy.

What is your attitude toward life? Is it the "illness" attitude? Do you believe that illness is just one of the natural accompaniments of living, that it is impossible to escape, that the "law of averages" makes your getting sick now and then inevitable, or that there are certain incurable diseases?

If you believe any or all of these, and at the same time want to get well, you will have to discard every one of them. You cannot stay well and maintain any part of the sick attitude.

You must be willing to accept the truth

—that health is natural, and illness is unnatural,
—that no one need ever be ill,
—that no disease is inevitable or incurable,
—and that if you *are* well you can *stay* well.

## The "Sickness" Order Needs Changing

Let us admit right now that, in the face of the sick attitudes which surround us, this is not easy.

Everywhere, billboards line our highways reminding us of our actual or potential ills. The radio is filled with recitations of impending epidemics, while bottled, boxed, and tubed weapons are urged upon us to do battle with them. Television gives us animated charts of various areas of the human body taking a beating just before some remedy comes charging on the scene to relieve it.

The demand for new angles has become so general, that certain television producers are growing desperate because their medical script-writers are running low on diseases. Writers are competing with one another to discover some new ailment they can bring before their public. Plot has become secondary to diseases that have not yet been tried on TV. No wonder a man once told me that before he began thinking creatively and positively, he could have started a drug-store with the contents of his medicine chest!

Today's children know more medical terms and the names of more maladies than many of the old respected country doctors whose patients often were healed through the ministrations of love and faith, when the contents of their little black bags had failed.

In many of our public schools children are taught the basic contents of first-aid kits, and sometimes are required to make up one of their own. There are gauze, adhesive-tape, alcohol, band-aids, aspirin, knife, scissors, matches, tincture of green soap, spirits of ammonia, needle and thread (not to mend the rip in a pair of pants, but to sew up some wound of the body), razor blades, safety pins, and merthiolate. About the only things overlooked are snake-bite remedies, syringes of morphine, and flasks of brandy.

The "sickness" attitude is rapidly becoming so old, so ingrained, so a part of our lives, that most men and women today are more familiar with the inside of a hospital than they are with the inside of a church. They've looked into the eyes of their doctors for physical answers more than they have into the eyes of their ministers for spiritual answers, upon which (they have forgotten) rests their entire physical world.

But this is an order which needs changing. It can be changed, however, only through these secrets of a new order which are accepted and acted upon by those who receive them.

This new order includes a terminology which substitutes words of health for words of illness; ideas of wholeness for fears of weakness and breakdown.

### Pack Your Own Healing Kit

But in spite of this constant education to sickness, each summer thousands of men and women go on vacations with no more protection than the ability to drive a car, a rudimentary knowledge of the rules of the road, a box of aspirin, crossed fingers, and the card of their insurance agent "in case they get involved in an accident." Others, however, lug along such a supply of medical aids that it takes an extra suitcase to carry them all. In addition, there are the required shots when they go abroad, and the travel insurance they buy in the waiting room before they take off.

In these secrets of healing and health, however, you have something which completely outclasses all other preventives, reliefs, treatments, and cures. It is a state of mind—the "wellness" attitude—backed by a consciousness of the spiritual power flowing constantly through your life.

Here is the greatest, most effective chest of mental and spiritual medicine you will ever find.

It needs no prescription except the knowledge of what it contains.

It costs nothing.

It weighs nothing.

You will have no trouble getting it through customs.

It cannot be left in the hotel-room 200 miles back down the road.

There is no bad taste in taking it.

There are no side-effects except good ones.

There is no cringing at the sight of a needle.

You will not need to hide it from the family or the authorities.

### You Don't Need to Bribe God

It is easy for the person who has health to forget the value of health. But when health is threatened or gone, an intense desire to be healed takes precedence over everything else. Seldom, if ever, do you hear someone say, "I'd sacrifice my health for money, place, position, power, happiness, success." But how often there is a willingness to sacrifice any or all of these for health itself.

Usually such willingness is expressed in some desperate plea to doctors, ministers, or practitioners. Often, as with the man on the roof, it takes the form of an even more desperate bribe to God. "O God," the ill person, says, "I'll sacrifice everything, I'll do anything you want, if only I can get well."

But why not get well and stay well without resorting to either bribes or desperation, neither of which has the slightest effect upon illness except to intensify it? No "sacrifice" in the old sense is necessary for healing or health. It is necessary only to give up some things in order to acquire others, no more than any of us do when we go to the store to buy something we desire. Our "giving up" is nothing more than an exchange or rearrangement of our values, practices, and beliefs. We give up, for instance, our warped, unsound, sick ideas, and acquire healthy new ones. We give up harmful practices and acquire helpful ones. We give up our false beliefs, and acquire true ones. We give up our fascination with the morbid and destructive things and conditions, and acquire an interest in the happy, constructive ones.

### Know the Truth About Yourself

Material riches, physical possessions, reputation, honor, power—all may go to make up the successful life. But important as these may be, they must not be considered more important than knowledge of ourselves and what makes us the way we are. Only by knowing the laws and potentials of our own being can we reach and maintain our health. The unknowing person is too prone to accept the facts of illness, pain, and suffering as either unavoidable or heroic only because he has no truth to explain his failure to make and keep his life well. If he stubbornly resists the acquisition of the knowledge that can save him, he will remain among the great majority of men and women who get well and fall ill with almost predictable regularity.

So long as any of us perpetuate our ignorance about ourselves, so long as our time is cut to pieces by dedicating it to weak acceptances of unnecessary illnesses and their causes, and to a belief in our helplessness or hopelessness—just so long will we be troubled, confused, unhappy, and ill.

### Begin Packing Now

If you truly want to get well and stay well, pack these truths and suggestions into your own spiritual-mental medicine kit, and take them with you for the remainder of your life:

1. The only true healing power there is, already is within your mind and your body. Everything else on the physical side is merely an ally on the physical level to hold in check the enemies of the senses and the attackers of the body, while the Great Physician—the healing power within you—goes to work. This healing power is available to you every second of your life. You need only follow these secrets of healing to have it demonstrate itself in your body.

2. See yourself whole, now and always. Do not hold before your mind's eye the image of yourself weak, ill, or helpless. Deny what you do not want; claim what you do. Identify yourself with yourself as a strong, well, perfect man or woman. Create a part and act that part in your imagination. Contemplate this image of yourself. Declare that it is true for you. The reality you claim in consciousness is the reality the world around you will begin to see and accept. Continue to see (in your imagination) only the condition of perfect health in you. Surround in consciousness the image of the person you want to be. This builds your faith in the reality of that image for you. Out of the former earthly illness, you will be building and preserving the spiritual temple of health.

3. Be worthy of the healing and the health you want. You cannot be negative and destructive in your thoughts, and expect your body to respond with strength, vigor, and perfect health. Unworthy thinking—thinking unworthy of the God in you—will "out." It will make itself known in ungodlike manifestations of the flesh. Healing and health are for those whose faith outweighs their fear, whose spiritual convictions overshadow their human uncertainties, and who are willing to know and to apply the secrets of the healing which lie waiting within themselves.

4. Whatever motives or justifications you may have for negative, destructive thinking; whatever "good reasons" you may have for getting angry, irritated, resentful, jealous, or hostile;

they can never be enough to warrant what such thinking does to you and your system. At all times, in all circumstances remember the theme of this book: "Think as if your life depends upon it, because it does."

5. Wherever you go, you will meet those whose ideas, philosophy, methods, ways, and motives conflict with yours. You may be inclined to strike back, to prove they are wrong, to argue, to be hurt, feel insulted, get angry. The only thing these reactions will ever gain for you is a little self-satisfaction that costs more than it is worth. It is quite easy to win a battle and lose a war. Good, strong, perfect cells are burnt up uselessly at times like this. What happens within you, within your own thinking, is far more important than what happens around you, or how someone else thinks. Jesus told us that it is not what comes to us, but what goes out from us that makes our life good or bad. It is not what others do, or fail to do, but how we react to what they do or fail to do that characterizes our lives. Take *that* capsule sometime when someone makes an unkind remark, when a member of the family criticizes or underestimates you, when someone thinks or acts contrary to your own wishes, when you feel your blood beginning to boil and sarcastic retorts framing themselves in your mind. It will do more toward calming your nerves and restoring your equilibrium and peace of mind than any tranquilizer ever made.

6. Whenever you have "emotional indigestion," you need regular capsule-meditations; that is, brief times of withdrawal from involvement with the world, into a state of mind where only truth and beauty are the objects of contemplation, and in which it becomes easy to release the emotional tensions that, unchecked, will wreck your life. In times of meditation, in moments of withdrawal, contemplate truth and beauty as you know it. Do not struggle with your thoughts. Think them quietly and easily.

7.  You may wonder whether you must, at some time, aban-
don all physical help, and rely solely upon the healing power
released by your own knowledge and faith. The answer depends
upon the level of that knowledge and faith. When it is high
and complete enough, no medical aids are necessary. When it is
not, no physical aid should be eliminated simply because it is
physical. God cannot be divided; the presence of the Infinite
is in everything. Everything is possible to God, but often we
allow our own human belief in limitation to block the possibilities. All things which help us are good. Do not stubbornly
insist on making yourself well by mental and spiritual help
alone, only to find that you are simply making yourself ill by
trying to force a spiritual law and power to work. It is only
pride that sometimes keeps the spiritually-minded from accepting the good that comes in physical form, yet pride will never
bring either healing or happiness. It has never brought it to us
in the past; it will not bring it to any of us in the future. However, to depend entirely upon physical help, to turn yourself
over completely to what can happen to you only through the
knife, the bottle, the pill, or the needle, is to renounce the truly
spiritual being you are to begin with, and to lose touch with
the healing power that waits for you only one thought away.

8.  Sometime there may come upon you the sickness of loneliness and fear, the feeling of desertion and rejection in an
indifferent world. You may feel inadequate to face a certain
challenge, or too weak to reach the goals of which you have
dreamed. For you at such times there is a four-word capsule
of truth which says, "You are never alone." Every person shares
in the presence of God. You have a great, silent partner who
never deserts you, who stands with you in times of triumph
and in hours of crisis. When life seems darkest, when discouragement settles upon you, when loneliness engulfs you,
or fear envelopes you, you can take that capsuled truth, "I am
never alone," and know that your recognition of this truth

will send new strength through you, give you new courage, sustain you until your desired world begins once again to manifest itself to you.

9. You are not here to convince God of anything. The only person who needs convincing of your health is yourself. Stop looking for an intercessor—someone to stand between you and God, someone to plead your case, someone to convince God that you are worthy of healing, someone to beg, plead or supplicate in your behalf. There need be no intercessor between you and God, because you are *in* God. "In God we live, and move, and have our being." You've heard it a thousand times. Have you really thought of what it means? The Infinite knows you are whole, perfect, incorruptible, well. It is only you who may begin to believe that you are corruptible, susceptible to illness, threatened by disease, ill. If you believe it, so you will be.

The secret challenge of the Garden of Eden was the discovery of our mind, a mind through which we were given the terrible power to choose between the false and the true. How easy it has been, through the evidence of our senses, to choose the false. We have used our minds to cram our thoughts full of the wrong things. In seeing the illness that is a reflection of our false beliefs, we have claimed the illness, and so strengthened the false beliefs. "I have arthritis." "My ulcers." "My weak back." "My bad eyes." "My poor feet." We are convincing ourselves we have an illness we do not want and are praying and paying to get rid of.

But here is the truth: God is already convinced that you are well. What are you waiting for? In God there is perfect harmony. This harmony is both the first and the ultimate state of life. When you are in harmony with life there can be only health. Therefore, it is the belief in this harmony in you and for you that you must acquire. This is the measure of your faith. If you believe that God can be ill, then there is little hope for you. If, however, you do not believe that God can be ill, then it remains for you only to orient yourself in terms of this perfection. Any beliefs in separation, illness, pain, or corruptibility must be released in the fact of the truth that you and God are not and cannot be separated. That which cannot happen to the Infinite cannot happen to you. The part cannot be different from the whole, unless it is separated from the whole. The only so-called separation is that which *seems* to occur when you *believe* in separation, when you believe that you somehow have splintered off from God, and are at the mercy of your own hostile environment and limited resources. It is such false beliefs which can be seen reflected in illness and disease.

It is not that you should be judged because of your illnesses, but only that you should be lifted above them, that you should give up your untruths for the truth. Re-orient yourself by coming into harmony with life, not by manufacturing and accepting all the excuses for your disharmonies. The true state, the end result, is this harmony with life, seeing and accepting yourself as part of a smooth-running, eternally-well, perfect life-force.

Recognize that when you are not well, you have simply let yourself drift from the center, and become influenced by the errors of the sensual world. Arrest that drift. Return to the center, and live in harmony with it. Do not go searching for the healing power in the shrines of this world. You carry it with you. It is released in you the moment you know and accept the truth. Do not search for the Guru, the healer, the priest, the minister, or the practitioner as an intercessor who can convince God that you ought to be healed, or that He should see that you stay well. Without your conscious or subconscious assent, there is absolutely no reason or power that can make you ill, or keep you ill. If you say, and believe, "In God we live and move and have our being," how can you possibly be ill?

# 17

## The Amazing Translation
## That Can Transform Your Life

The great masterpieces of literature such as *The Odyssey,*
*Faust, The Brothers Karamazov, War and Peace, Remembrance
of Things Past,* and *The Divine Comedy,* have been translated
into almost every one of the world's major languages.

Although every translator tells the story of the original, the
translations are different, each according to the understanding
and ability of the translator. Some, coming close to the original,
are powerful, expressive, and beautiful. Some are weak, uneven,
and inaccurate. Others are down-right failures. The original is
the masterpiece. The translations are attempts to equal it in
another language. No translator wants to do a bad job. He wants
his translation to be as close to the original masterpiece as
possible.

So, in terms of life, the perfect masterpiece is God, the
Creator, the Infinite. Use whatever term you wish. Every life
is a translation; every experience in that life is a chapter. The
translator is our own consciousness. Whether that translation
is a good one, whether it accurately transmutes the life of God

into the life of man, whether it is a much abridged edition with limitations and deletions, or whether it is halting, uneven, imperfect, and a failure, depends upon the understanding and ability of the mind which achieved it. It is an understanding of our own inner powers which will help us translate the Infinite masterpiece into a satisfying life-experience for us.

These final words, which are intended to help you stay well, concern that most amazing translation—the human body. I would like to speak of it not in medical or scientific terms, but in terms of everyday experience and understanding, so that together we can contemplate it as the truly remarkable translation it is. Just as we take the letters of the alphabet and create word-forms that may be translated into other languages, so we take our perceptions, talents, abilities, powers, and tendencies, and create thought-forms (idea-, belief-, fear-, and attitude-forms) that in a subconscious way we immediately begin translating into physical (body) forms.

At the same time that we are translating the original masterpiece into our individual lives, we are re-translating that individual life into a three-dimensional form called the body. Granted, we have been given a body that is more or less standardized. We have this to start with. But the poet, too, for instance, is given a standardized form called the sonnet. It is what he creates within the framework of that sonnet form which will determine not merely its form, but its quality. It will tell whether that sonnet is good or bad, beautiful or ugly, powerful or weak. There is a tremendous difference between the sonnets of Keats, Shelley, William Shakespeare, or Elizabeth Barrett Browning, and those of a thousand John Does who try to write them. The form may be the same, but the quality and content are not.

We are given a mind, a form as physically rigid and meticulous as a sonnet or a symphony, as a statue or a play, but it is our handling of that form—what we create within that framework—which will tell the quality of that which inevitably will be translated into our body. Unlike the poet who chose to be a poet, the composer who chose to be a composer, the playwright who chose to be a playwright, the novelist who chose to be a novelist, the sculptor who chose to be a sculptor— we did not choose to be a person. The choice was made for us even before we arrived. We began as an unwitting translator of our thoughts into body-form.

We do not need to belabor the point that we are what we think, and that the body is a reflection of what we are. Even now, given the illnesses, diseases, accidents, troubles, and problems of a person's life, any good practitioner of psychosomatic medicine or science of mind can draw up a fairly accurate description of the thinking, of the mental, emotional, and spiritual condition of that person. So long as he gets an accurate list, he will know the areas of weakness in that person's life, even though he does not know the person himself. All this goes back to that remarkable sentence from the book of John: "...the word was made flesh, and dwelt among us." Our thoughts, attitudes, ideas, fears, emotions, and beliefs become flesh in ways we sometimes never guess.

It is common enough to hear someone say, "I just made myself sick with worry," or "I worried myself sick!" The worry, of course, was translated into illness. Since this is so common, and since almost everyone agrees that the result of worry can be and often is illness, isn't it strange that we do not hear anyone say, "I made myself well with creative, healing thinking," or "I thought myself well." For the truth is that *creative thinking translates itself into health just as readily as negative (worried) thinking translates itself into illness.* Why, then, do we not hear such a statement, except possibly from those who know and practice the principles and truths revealed in this book? Because so few men and women ever learn the truth that they have a healing power, as well as a destructive power, within their own mind; that the body responds according to the kind of thinking they do. With every thought they are translating inner power into outer form.

For those who can read the signs, each one of us is a walking advertisement for the kind of translation he is making. Although we were born into this world the unwitting translator of our thoughts into body-states and conditions, we do not need to remain that unwitting translator. The process of translation continues despite us, so we may as well start making it produce pleasant, acceptable, desirable results.

If every thought we had, every belief we held, were written down and then translated into all the world's languages, to be posted on some public bulletin-board, you can be quite sure we would watch and discipline our thinking more carefully. Yet, every thought we have, every belief we hold is noted in the mysterious bulletin-board of the subconscious, and posted, often conspicuously, in the body. How is it, then, that we are so careless about watching and disciplining those thoughts? Is it because the private pain is easier to bear than the public embarrassment? This may be part of it, but there seems to be an even more subtle reason. It is because the translation of thought into form is such a slow process that the thinker seldom connects the thought with the subsequent pain. The translation usually takes time, and by the time it is finished, the translator has forgotten what started it all.

These final words, then, are to remind you—the thinker—that the process of translation is going on whether you know it or like it; that you had best learn something about the rhythm, meter, and laws of that sonnet called your mind so that you will not bungle the job you are called upon to do, and end with a translation unworthy of the Creator of that masterpiece with which you began.

Today, somewhere, a belief in separation will be translated into a broken bone.

Somewhere else the attitude of hatred and hostility will be translated into a stroke.

Over the years, extended feelings of loss, rejection, or unworthiness, or of futility, hopelessness, and depression may be translated into leukemia and cancer.

Tension and irritation find their physical form in ulcers, stomach trouble, and kidney disease.

Somewhere a sense of "overload," a belief in burdens too heavy to bear, is being translated into backache, headache, heart trouble, muscle-spasms, and organic break-downs.

Somewhere the feeling of restriction and limitation, the belief in the status-quo simply because it is the status-quo, the emotion of resentment and irritation are all being translated into arthritis, bursitis, and rheumatism.

The translations are all around us and in us, yet we so often fail to realize what they are. We attribute our illnesses and difficulties to so many things other than ourselves. We are part of a vast library of translations. Back of them and responsible for them are the thoughts, attitudes, ideas, fear, emotions, and beliefs of those minds which they represent.

Is your translation adequate, desirable, worthy, healthy, vigorous? If not—if it is poor, weak, sickly, uncertain, incompetent—what can you do about it? The answer is an easy one if you will apply yourself, remembering that sentence, ". . . the word was made flesh, and dwelt among us."

Keep that "word" within you strong, confident, positive, creative, thankful.

Remember to use the kind of material for your translation that will make it what you want it to be.

Allow yourself none of the ideas, attitudes, emotions, or beliefs that have no choice but to manifest themselves in weakness and ill health.

It is more than a moral issue; it is an issue of health or illness, strength or weakness, life or death. If you want to stay well, you must use only positive, healing, loving, faith-filled materials for that most amazing translation—your body.

John Donne carried this idea of translation one step further. It seems appropriate to quote him as we reach the end of this book:

> All mankind is of one Author, and is one volume. When one man dies, one chapter is not torn out of the book, but translated into a better language, and every chapter must be so translated. God employs several translators. Some pieces are translated by age, some by sickness, some by war, some by justice. But God's hand is in every translation, and His hand shall bind up all our scattered leaves again for that library where every book shall lie open one to the other.